The
Universal Dream Book

by

ZADKIEL

THE BOOK TREE
San Diego, California

Originally published
circa 1850
by W. Nicholson & Sons, Ltd.
London

New material, revisions and cover
© 2008
The Book Tree
All rights reserved

ISBN 978-1-58509-326-7

Cover layout and design
by Toni Villalas

Published by
The Book Tree
P.O. Box 16476
San Diego, CA 92176
www.thebooktree.com

We provide fascinating and educational products to help awaken the public to new ideas and
information that would not be available otherwise.
Call 1 (800) 700-8733 for our *FREE BOOK TREE CATALOG*.

Foreword

The interpretation of dreams goes far back into human history. For as long as we have been having dreams, mankind has been attempting to decipher them. Dreams are often considered important, powerful omens as evidenced by their many appearances in the Bible and in other religions worldwide. A favorite for more than century, *The Universal Dream Book* is now available once again. Zadkiel, whose real name was Richard James Morrison, lived in London in the 1800's and was one of the first astrologers to be published for the masses. He created an astrological yearbook and due to his popularity, "Zadkiel's Almanac" consistently sold in the thousands.

This is his legendary book of dreams, important today on a number of levels. He takes the most common dream symbols of his time and lists them in order, alphabetically. It is, in effect, a dream dictionary. It accurately reveals what many symbols, animals and events truly mean when we dream them. It also allows us to take a trip back in time to see what people were dreaming about most of the time in the 1800's, and allows us to compare that with today. Many things we dream about will never change, and these we will instantly recognize and learn about in the book. But the things that do change in the dream world allow us to see what consciousness has considered important in the past but, for some reason, has excluded from our collective consciousness of the present. This book is highly recommended for those engaged in dream research, or for those of us who wish to explore the inner world for ourselves.

Paul Tice

DREAMS
AND THEIR INTERPRETATIONS.

ABANDON.—To dream that you abandon a person, is unfavourable; it intimates that you will lose friendships and favours which it will be very difficult to recover.—To dream that you are abandoned, denotes coming trouble.

ABBEY.—This denotes future comfort, peace of mind, freedom from anxiety.

ABDICATE.—To dream of a monarch abdicating his throne in any kingdom denotes anarchy and revolution there.

ABHOR.—To dream you are abhorred, not liked, and if you are troubled at the same, some enemies will injure you; if in your dream you are not troubled thereby, but rather defiant, it is a sign that you will surmount all opposition, and triumph over all your foes.

ABJECT.—Dreaming that you are in a forlorn and abject state, I fear, indicates coming poverty; if, in your dream, you appear cheerful under it, it will only be for a season, and prosperity will succeed.

ABORTION.—If a male dreams of this, trouble is approaching the partner of his life. If a female dreams of this, it is a dream of *caution;* beware; guard your health, or a sad calamity will ensue.

ABROAD.—To dream of being abroad, in a foreign country, denotes a change in your situation in life; you are likely to be unsettled in life, and to change your locality.

ABSCOND.—To dream that you abscond, or run away, is a sign that you are in danger of acting dishonourably; therefore, beware. If you dream of another person absconding; you will meet with a treacherous person—an unfaithful friend. Therefore, be on the look out. For a female to dream that her lover has absconded, is a sure sign that another possesses her heart, and vice versa.

ABSENT FRIENDS.—To dream of absent friends and that they are alive, but ill, indicates hasty intelligence, of a disagreeable nature; to dream that they are well denotes they are in a prosperous state, and that their friendship to you abides; to dream of the death of some absent friend foretells good news relating to a wedding.

ABSTAIN.—To dream that you are a total abstainer, denotes good health, success in life; great prosperity.

ABUNDANCE.—Dreaming of abundance denotes success in your plans, and a pleasing competence in life in consequence.

ABUSE.—To dream that some one is abusing you is a sure sign that you will quarrel with your lover, or your friend, and that some one has been speaking ill of you. In trade it indicates a great loss and often a robbery, therefore take care of your money. It would be as well also to be careful, when you retire to rest, of your fires and lights, as it often indicates loss of life and property by fire.

ABUSE.—To dream that you are abused and insulted, denotes that a dispute will arise between you and some one with whom you do business. If you are in love, be sure that some one has attempted to injure you with the object of your love, and is likely to succeed. Take heed, and be not slack in your attentions to your lover.

ABYSS.—Trouble, trouble is coming. You will be in straits and difficulties most formidable and from which it will be difficult for your friends to extricate you.

ACADEMY.—To dream that you are master, or mistress of an academy, indicates that you will be reduced in your circumstances; if single, that your intended marriage will be characterized by adversity.

ACCIDENT.—Dreaming that you meet with an accident to the injury of any part of your body, denotes coming personal affliction; but from which you will recover. To dream of an accident at sea, you will be crossed in love.

ACCUSE.—To dream that you are accused of a crime of which you are guilty, is a sign of great trouble, to dream that you are not found guilty, it denotes the failure of your enemy's evil designs, and that you will rise superior to all evil machinations. It denotes that you will acquire riches, by your own personal efforts, aided by the gifts of your friends.

ACHE.—To dream that you have aches and pains, denote a temporary illness, and some slight troubles.

ACORNS.—When you dream of acorns, it is a good sign; it betokens health, strength, and worldly abundance; if single, you are likely to marry well, and have a numerous and agreeable family. To a married woman it denotes the birth of twins. To tradesmen it is the omen of prosperity and wealth; and to all it is a good sign. To the lover it denotes success and happiness. To those in difficulties, a speedy deliverance.

ACQUAINTANCE.—To dream of an acquaintance, denotes his or their continued friendship. It is a sign that they are sincere.

ACQUIT.—To dream that you are charged with offence before a tribunal, and acquitted for want of evidence, is a sure sign of the utter confusion of your enemies, and of your own prosperity and stability.

ADMIRE.—To dream that you admire a person is an omen that your partner loves you, without ostentation; and if single, that your lover is sincere. To dream that you are admired betokens numerous friends.

ADULTERY.—Dreaming of being tempted to commit this crime, and of a successful resistance of it, intimates that in future life virtue will be your guide, and that you will greatly prosper; that your schemes and plans admirably succeed. But if you dream of being guilty of the vice, it is a sad omen of approaching troubles; that your prospects in love will be blasted, while despair will wring your heart with anguish.

ADVANCEMENT.—If you dream that you are advanced in your situation, it is a sign of success in all you undertake; if you are single, that your lover will be sincerely devoted to you. Altogether it is a favourable sign. If engaged in a law-suit, or any dispute, it is a sign that you will win.

ADVERSARY.—To dream you meet with an adversary, denotes that you will overcome some obstacle to your happiness; it denotes that your affairs will prosper, though you have enemies. If soliciting a situation, you will meet with impediments, yet you will overcome them.

ADVERSITY.—To dream of being in adverse circumstances is always a favourable dream ; It generally indicates the reverse, prosperity.

> "Content and happy may they be
> Who dream of cold adversity ;
> To married man and married wife
> It promises a happy life,
> With many children, many friends ;
> While unto others it portends
> Success in love, success in trade,
> A husband to the blooming maid
> The farmer may expect each field
> A full abundant crop to yield ;
> The hardy sailor is sure to find
> On his next voyage a favouring wind
> And all will surely happy be
> Who dream of cold adversity."

ADVICE.—To dream that you are receiving advice, denotes difficulties ; but you will have wise and faithful friends to help you. To dream that you are giving advice, is a sign that you will be highly esteemed by your friends and acquaintances.

ADVOCATE.—To dream that you are an advocate, or that you are advocating the cause of some one, is a sign that your future station will be a prominent one, and that for benevolent purposes, which will crown you with high honour, and gain you universal respect.

AFFILIATION.—To dream that you have a child fathered on you is a very bad dream, it indicates dreadful enemies, and a long and severe illness or else a sudden death. If you are about to make a journey by land or a voyage by sea, abandon it for some time to come, for it will prove an unfortunate one to you; such a dream always foretells the loss of life or limb. For a young woman to dream that she is fathering a child on some one, implies that her life is actuated by improper motives, and if he cannot secure his object he will abandon her.

AFFLICTION.—It denotes a change of residence; to the young and single early marriage, but not agreeable. It is not a good omen. It indicates trouble.

AFFLUENCE.—To dream of affluence is not very favourable. It has frequently been found to denote the contrary.

AFFRONT.—To dream that you are affronted by a person denotes disappointment in love, and trouble and vexation through one that owes you money; in every case you will find it the forerunner of annoyance and discontent.

AFRAID.—This goes by the contrary. It denotes that in future trials you will be valiant, and not afraid. That your cause will succeed. That your lover will prove true.

AGE.—A dream about your age betokens sickness, and premature death.

AGUE.—To dream that you have the ague denotes constant changes in your business and circumstances. They will alternate; sometimes you will be prosperous, then poor. To dream that you and your lover have both the ague, prognosticates that the connection will be dissolved.

ALEHOUSE.—If you dream you are in an alehouse, it denotes that you will be exposed to the malice of low mean enemies. If a female dreams she is in an alehouse, it is a sign that her future husband will love his cups. To dream that you are drinking ale with companions, denotes deception by the flatterer.

ALIEN.—To dream that you are an alien, or alienated, is a dream of contrary — the reverse will take place; abiding friendship and love.

ALLIGATOR.—This denotes a sly crafty enemy; and such a dream should excite to caution.

ALMONDS.—To dream of eating sweet almonds indicates future enjoyment, probably by travel in a distant country. If you relish the almonds, every undertaking nearly will be prosperous; if the taste is bitter, your enterprise will fail; and the expenses of it will nearly overwhelm you.

ALTAR.—To dream you are at the altar, and receiving the holy sacrament, is a very unfavourable omen, denoting many heavy and severe afflictions. If you are in love, your lover will be taken away by death, or removed very far from you for ever. If in business, losses will be yours.

AMPUTATION.—To dream that you are having a limb cut off is a certain warning of the death of some near and dear object, wife or husband, child, parent or lover. Bereavement must certainly be your lot.

ANCHOR.—To dream of an anchor in water is a bad omen, it implies disappointment in your wishes and endeavours. To dream of an anchor part in water and part out, foretells that you will speedily have a voyage. For a young woman to dream of an anchor she will have a sailor for her husband. For a woman with child to dream of an anchor she will have a son and he will be a sailor. To dream you

see an anchor difficult to weigh is a good sign denoting your abiding prosperity, and the futility of all
opposition from your enemies.

ANGELS.—This is a pleasing and favourable dream.
It is a sign of high enjoyment. If you dream you
are with them, it indicates that you will have sweet
fellowship with agreeable friends; that you will have
prosperity, peace, and happiness. To a married woman it denotes she will have a numerous and virtuous family; if she dream of two angels, she will have
twins the next birth. It is a happy omen to lovers;
their marriage will be agreeable, and they will be surrounded with kind friends.

ANGER.—To dream you are angry with some person, it is a sign that that person is your best friend.
Should you dream that your lover is angry with you
be assured they love you sincerely and will make you
happy.

ANGLING.—This dream betokens much affliction
and trouble in your life engagements. I fear too it
indicates sophistry, and design to entangle some in
your meshes. Do not be guilty of such conduct.
Resist the temptation that you may be delivered from
evil.

ANNOY.—To dream that you are annoyed denotes
that you have enemies about you.

ANTS.—Dreaming of ants it foretells your removal
to a large mercantile city where you will have a
numerous family of boys; that if you are industrious
you may accumulate riches; but if not, you will live
in poverty. To those in love it foretells a speedy
marriage, and a large family. It intimates to the

tradesman increase of trade and ultimate independence.

ANXIETY.—It is a dream of contrary, and denotes that your present trouble and anxiety will soon pass away.

APPAREL.—To dream that you have good rich apparel, is a dream of contrary; indicating want and penury, and great scarcity of clothes. If you dream you have no clothes is also a dream of contrary; you will have a sufficiency, if not more, of temporal things, and many changes of raiment.

APPAREL,—WHITE.—To dream you are robed in white is a sure token of your success with a lover; of success in business, or any honourable undertaking, you will find great favour with the public.

APPAREL,—BLACK.—If you go to a funeral in black, it denotes a marriage in which you and your friends are interested. But to dream of black apparel on ordinary occasions is unlucky. It denotes sickness to yourself, or family, and you will be bereaved of some one dear to you. Engage not in law-suits, for your dream portends evil, embarrassment, and difficulties; and go not any journey, for it may be unsuccessful. Are you a lover? It denotes that the object of your devotion is in trouble, unhappy, or afflicted, and likely to pay the debt of nature soon.

APPAREL,—BLUE OR PURPLE.—Denotes prosperity, happiness, and esteem, from various persons whom you wish to please. Your sweetheart is by this colour denoted very faithful, and if you marry the object of your wishes, you will experience great happiness and comfort; great success in business, approbation of friends, and much advantage by travelling.

APPAREL,—SCARLET.—By dreaming of this colour you are warned that you will experience heavy calamities, sickness, loss of friends, quarrels and disputes, originating in mere trifles; it also denotes great uneasiness by the misconduct of children.

To dream of being dressed in CRIMSON denotes that the dreamer will live to an old age, and have a moderate fortune through life; you are about to receive some pleasant news from a distant quarter; your sweetheart will leave you for some time, but afterwards will be very faithful to you.

To dream you are dressed in a variety of colours, denotes a variety of fortune will attend you. If you are in love, a quarrel will take place between you and your sweetheart, which, after some uneasiness will be settled by friends.

To dream you see another in any of the modes above described, forebodes to the party the same fortune.

To dream you are dressed in new clothes, is a favourable sign; it portends honour and success in your undertakings.

APPLES.—This is a very good dream; it indicates a long and happy life, success in business and in love. For a woman with child to dream of apples denotes that she will have a son who will be very great and wealthy.

ARROW.—To dream that an arrow is shot at you, and that it penetrates your body is a bad omen. Some person or persons are designing your ruin.

ASCEND.—To dream that you ascend a hill, and

reach the top, denotes that you will conquer your difficulties.

ASPS.—To dream of asps is a sure sign of enemies. If you dream that you tread upon them do not fear, they cannot injure you. If they run from you, you will triumph over them, but if they turn and bite you, it denotes dangerous enemies who will greatly injure you, and cause you much trouble.

ASS.—This denotes that whatever troubles or misfortunes at present afflict you, will, by patience and humility, sustain them, and that they will have a happy termination. For a young woman to dream of an ass implies that her future husband will be contented and happy, but not rich, rather headstrong, and determined to have his own way.

ASYLUM.—To dream that you are in an asylum denotes coming personal affliction. But to dream that you are merely inspecting an asylum, denotes that you will be in circumstances that will enable you to help the distressed.

BABY.—To dream that you are nursing a baby denotes sorrow and misfortune, and disappointment in love. To dream that you see a baby that is sick, foretells the death of one of the family. For a young woman to dream of having a baby, implies that she is in danger of temptation, and that she will be forsaken by her lover, and for a young man to dream that he is married, and is nursing a baby, denotes disappointment in the object of his affections, perhaps by her death.

BACHELOR.—Dreaming of a bachelor not old; portends that you will shortly meet with a lover, or friend. But to dream that you converse with an old bachelor is a sign that you are likely to die an old maid.

BACON.—To dream of eating bacon portends sorrow. To dream of buying it foretells the death of a friend, or that you will quarrel with your lover and part for ever. It predicts great trials by sickness.

BADGER.—If you dream of this animal, it is a favourable circumstance, it indicates long life and great prosperity, that you will acquire wealth by your industry, and that you will have to travel much in your own and foreign countries.

BAGPIPES.—This musical instrument seen and heard in a dream, always denotes extreme poverty, and that you will have to labour hard all your life. It also denotes that the marriage state will be unhappy, as your wife will be proud and over-bearing and not very industrious. Your marriage state will be full of cares, and very bitter.

BAKING.—To dream of baking bread, denotes sorrow, and a death in the family; or if a young person, the death or serious illness of your intended. To dream of baking pies, tarts, &c., denotes that you are to assist at a wedding, or you will be called upon to be married yourself very soon.

BALL.—If you dream that you see persons dance at a ball, and that you are engaged yourself, signifies joy, recreations, and good fellowship. It denotes the reception of a large sum of money, or very favourable intelligence. In matters of love, it foretells happiness and success, and that you will have a large family of boys and girls, which will be a comfort to you.

BALD.—To dream of baldness portends approaching sickness. For a young woman to dream that her lover is bald, foretells that he will not live to marry her. To dream that she is bald herself, implies she will be very poor, and die an old maid.

BANKRUPT.—To dream of insolvency is a dream of warning, lest you should undertake something discreditable and injurious to yourself, and opposed to the approbation of your friends. Therefore be cautious in your transactions and conduct, enter into no hasty contracts either in business or love, but seek the advice of your friends, for a step imprudently taken may embitter your future life.

BASIN.—To dream you are eating or drinking out of a basin, denotes that you will soon be in love; but without great care you will not marry the first object of your affections.

BATS.—To dream of seeing a bat flying in the air signifies that you have an enemy. If it appears flying by daylight you need not fear, but if by night, you are in danger. For a young person in love to dream of a bat denotes that you will have a dangerous rival to annoy you.

BATHING.—If you dream that you are bathing, and that the water is clear and transparent, prosperity and success in business, and in love will be yours; but if the water be dirty and muddy, you will have nothing but poverty, misfortune, sorrow, and very poor health.

BATTLE.—To dream of being in a battle implies disagreement with neighbours or friends, and with your lover of a serious nature. For a married person to dream of a battle, denotes future difficulty in obtaining temporal supplies. But if you overcome in battle, it indicates that you will baffle all the attempts of your enemies to injure you, and that success in business will be yours. In love-affairs your wishes will be realized.

BEANS.—To dream of beans is unfortunate. If you dream of eating them it foretells sickness. If you dream of seeing them growing, it foretells contention with those you love best.

BEAR.—To dream of seeing a bear, expect great vexations, and that some despotic enemy will injure you ; and that if you travel, you will meet with great hardships, but the end of your journey will be safely accomplished, and the intent accomplished. To dream that you are fighting with a bear, and kill it, is a favourable sign of your overcoming a formidable foe.

BEAUTY.—To dream that you are beautiful, is a dream of contrary, denoting that sickness will spoil your countenance, and debilitate your strength. To dream of any friend as beautiful, denotes their sickness. If you see your own and their beauty increase, it denotes death.

BED.—To dream of being in bed signifies a very early marriage to yourself; and to dream of making a bed indicates a change of residence, and that you will live from home a long time. To dream of sitting upon a maid's bedside is certainly a sign of marriage.

BEEF.—To dream of eating beef indicates that you will always live in plenty, though you may not be rich ; but to dream of beef, and that you have not the power to eat it denotes that you will be dependent on another's bounty.

BEES.—To dream of bees is good; it denotes that your industry and enterprise in trade will be very successful. In all states of life, to dream of these insects is a good omen; to the rich, it denotes dignity and honour, and to the poor success, and a comfortable competency. To the lover it indicates happy wedlock with a virtuous, industrious, and amiable person; also it denotes a numerous family of industrious habits and amiable dispositions, proving a blessing to their parents in their declining years, and not a curse.

To dream of bees is a rare good sign,
For wealth and great pleasure shall be thine;
Free shalt thou be from poverty's pain,
All things tending to give thee gain.

Look forward with joy to this blest state
Of honour, and peace, and riches great;
Work on, hope on, trusting in heaven,
And all this good to thee shall be given.

Thy wife shall become a fruitful vine;
Children around thee in virtue shall shine;
Thy life shall pass unmingled with care;
Thy dreaming of bees denotes such fare.

BELLS.—To dream of hearing the bells ring is a fortunate sign. It is a sign of coming good news. To the young it foretells a happy and early marriage to the person so ardently loved by them. To persons in business it denotes the acquirement of a fortune. It foretells advancement in your trade or profession. If a sailor at sea dreams of hearing the bells, it augurs that his voyage will be prosperous, and that he will safely return, and marry well.

BILLIARDS.—If you dream that you are playing at billiards, it indicates that you will be placed in a difficult position, from which it will be hard to extricate yourself. If you are courting a young lady, it denotes that you will be opposed by her parents or friends.

BIRDS.—For a wealthy person to dream of birds flying, is very unlucky, it denotes a sad reverse in their circumstances. But for poor persons to dream of birds it denotes a change for the better, especially if they hear the birds singing. If the birds have a beautiful plumage, and are not frightened at you, it indicates elevation to rank and influence.

BIRD'S NEST.—To dream of finding a bird's nest containing eggs, is a sign that you will have property left. If there are young ones in, you will have a lawsuit about it and lose it.

BIRTH.—For a married woman to dream of giving birth to a child portends that she will get well over her confinement. For a single young woman to dream the same denotes that she is in danger of losing her chastity.

BLACKBERRIES.—To dream that you are gathering blackberries to eat, indicates approaching sickness. If you see others gathering them, you have enemies where you least expect them, and who will strive to injure you in your business.

BLEEDING.—To dream of bleeding in any part of your person is a very unhappy dream; especially if you dream it cannot be stopped; it is the sign of protracted illness, and debility through life.

BLIND.—For persons in love to dream that they are blind, denotes that they have made a bad choice in the object of their affections; and that their connection will by some unexpected cause come to an end. To dream of the blind is a sign that you will have few real friends.

BLOOD.—To dream of blood is very bad, if you see it upon yourself; if on others, it denotes a sudden death to some of the family, loss of property, and severe disappointment. If expecting to be married, something will occur to prevent your union, and if you dream that your hands are bloody, you will be in danger of injuring some person. Beware!

BOAT.—If you dream that you are sailing in a boat or ship and the water is smooth and the weather pleasant, it is a lucky omen, denoting a prosperous business, and happiness in the marriage state. If the water is rough and muddy you will have to labour all your life. If you fall into the water you will meet hereafter with great peril.

BONES.—Dreaming of bones denotes poverty; if they are partly clothed with flesh, that you will grow rich by degrees, and ultimately possess a good deal of property. To dream of human bones foretells that you will become rich through the death of some relative or friend.

BOOKS.—To dream of books is a good sign; it denotes that your future life will be very agreeable. If a woman in the family way dreams that she sees a number of books, it betokens the birth of a son who will rise to eminent learning and great honour. For young woman to dream of books indicates that she will be married to a very learned man.

BOOTS.—If you dream that you are wearing a new pair of boots and they hurt your feet, it is a sign that you will meet with great and painful difficulties caused by your own imprudence.

BOTTLE.—To dream of a bottle full of wine indicates your future prosperity; if the bottle be empty, it denotes that you have an enemy in possession of a secret, which if revealed, will do you a deal of harm. To dream that you are drinking out of a bottle denotes that you are intending mischief on some young person, and which, if perpetrated will greatly injure your character.

BOWER.—To dream you are seated in a bower portends that you will overcome every obstacle to your happiness. If in a bower with your lover, indicates that your lover is sincere and faithful; speedy marriage, and great happiness in that state.

BOW AND ARROW.—To dream that you are shooting with a bow and arrow, and that you hit the target, denotes that your future well-organized plans will succeed above all you could have imagined; if you miss the target, that your schemes are not well organized, and that the object of your ambition will be blasted. If a young woman dreams that her lover is shooting with a bow and arrow, it foretells her that he is a restless fickle being, always changing his plans and pursuits, to gain money which he will never acquire.

BOX.—If you dream that you are opening a box, and looking for something in it, and cannot find it, it is an indication that you are going to be troubled about money matters; or that you will suffer some pecuniary lost.

BOX.—To dream of the plant "Box," implies long life and prosperity, with a happy marriage and large family, to be your solace in old age.

BRACELET.—To dream that you are wearing a

bracelet, you will shortly be married to a wealthy person. If you dream that you find a bracelet it is a sign of a coming fortune; if you dream that some one put upon your hand a bracelet you will soon fall in love, and be accepted, or if already in love, you will be married without delay.

BRAMBLES.—To dream of briars and brambles and that you are injured by them, is a very unlucky dream, it denotes many difficulties, and poverty and privation all your life. If you are not hurt by them, you will have trouble but of a short duration.

BRANCH.—If you dream that you see a tree full of branches, it denotes abundance, and a numerous family,—a happy posterity.

BREAD.—To dream of seeing a quantity of bread is a sign of competency in temporal things. If you dream of eating good bread, you will enjoy good health, and live long; but if the bread is burned or sad, it is a bad sign, and generally portends a funeral. To dream of baking bread is also bad, generally denoting affliction, and sorrow.

TO BREAK.—To dream of any breakage is unlucky. If you dream of breaking any of your limbs it is a sign of approaching sickness. If you dream of breaking tables or chairs, or any article of furniture, it indicates insolvency. If you dream of breaking a window, it forebodes a robbery, or danger from fire. If you dream of breaking a looking glass, it implies the death of a relative, neighbour, or friend. To dream of breaking earthenware or glass, denotes a robbery by a servant; and if a woman dreams of breaking her wedding-ring it portends the death of her husband.

BREAST.—To dream that you are reclining on the breast of another, is a sign of true, valuable, lasting friendship, and affection.

BREATH.—To dream you are out of breath, or have difficult breathing is a sign that your health is about to give way.

BREWING.—If you dream that you are brewing, you may expect the visit of some distant friend. It denotes also great efforts to secure your honourable purposes, and that you shall succeed, and for a short time have both trouble and uneasiness, but all will end happily.

BRIDE, BRIDESMAID, OR BRIDEGROOM.—This is a dream of contrary. To dream that you take any of these characters is very unlucky, it is a sure fore-runner of grief and disappointment, and that the dreamer will soon have to be chief mourner at a funeral of some dear friend, or acquaintauce.

BRIDGE.—To dream that you are crossing a bridge in the day time, foretells a change of situation. If any person interrupts you, it implies that your lover will deceive you; but if you pass along without any impediment, you will succeed in your undertakings, and prosper. If you dream that you are walking towards a bridge that is broken down, be not hasty to make any change in your situation for the present, as you will not be successful.

BUGLE.—To dream that you are playing this in-strument, is a token of joy, occasioned by great friend-ship and kindness from your relatives. To dream of hearing a bugle sound denotes unexpected news from abroad of a very pleasing nature; and to married persons it denotes the birth of a child.

BUGS.—To dream of these filthy vermin, is a sure indication of sickness, and of many enemies seeking to injure you. To a young man it implies that his enemies are trying to deprive him of his situation. To a young woman, that she has several rivals who do not hesitate to traduce her character. To a merchant or tradesman, it denotes that he has servants or persons in his employment who are robbing him, and injuring him to a great extent.

BUILDINGS.—If you dream of seeing a large number of new buildings, it indicates that you will shortly remove to a distant place, where you will be far happier, and escape the design of some secret enemies. If the buildings are large and magnificent, you will be prosperous and happy; If they are palaces, it prognosticates much wealth and honour. But if they appear small, mean, and dilapidated, your circumstances will be indigent. If the buildings are only partly built, and you inquire why they are not finished, and no one can tell you, it is a sign that your plans are difficult to accomplish, and that you will die while they are incomplete.

BULL.—To dream that you are pursued by a mad bull, denotes that you have violent enemies, and that many injurious reports will be spread detrimental to your character; and that you will be in danger of losing your friends. If in love, your intended will be in some great danger, and will narrowly escape some dreadful misfortune.

BURNS.—A dream of contrary, implying health, happiness and warm friendship.

BUTTER.—To dream of butter, in any way, or form, is a good dream and indicates joy and feasting. To the lover it is a sign of early marriage. In litigation it betokens success; also in any controversy, or dispute. Your absent friend, if you have one, will come home safely, and be to you a friend in need. If you are exposed to any trial or danger, it betokens speedy deliverance.

BUTTER-MILK.—To dream of drinking butter-milk implies that your intended has but an irritable and unamiable temper, or that you will be disappointed in love; that your rival will take your lover from you. To a married person it denotes losses, sorrow and mourning. To a farmer, an uncongenial season, and loss of crops, if he dreams of seeing butter-milk in large quantities it indicates losses, but that he will overcome them.

CABBAGE.—To dream of cutting cabbages denotes that your wife, or lover, or husband, as the case may be, is very jealous of you. If you dream of some one else cutting them, it is a sign that you have an enemy trying to create jealousy in the mind of your beloved. If you dream of eating cabbage, it denotes the sickness of the object of your affections, and that you will have severe losses and loss of a sum of money.

CAB.—To dream of riding in a cab denotes a short sickness, and speedy recovery by change of climate. It also denotes increasing prosperity.

CAGE.—To dream that you see birds in a cage is a sign that you will have an early and an agreeable marriage. If you dream you see a cage, the door open, and no bird there, it is a sign that your lover will forsake you; and it is much if ever you be married. To dream of seeing a person letting a bird escape from its cage, is a sign of an elopement.

CAKES.—If you dream of oat-cakes, it denotes health and strength; if of sweet cakes, of coming joy; if of making spicy cakes and bread, an approaching marriage, at which you will be, and meet with your lover who will receive you with open arms. To dream of cakes twice, denotes your own marriage in which you will be happy both day and night.

CALM.—To dream of a calm succeeding a storm indicates the reconciliation of separated friends; the end of trouble; the commencement of peace.

CALUMNY.—To dream that you are calumniated, is a dream of contrary, denoting that you will be generally and highly respected.

CAMELS.—To dream of these wonderfully hard and patient creatures, denotes that heavy burdens will press upon you, that you will be hardly dealt with, meet with many disasters, all which you will bear with heroism; but the time will come when you will be entirely emancipated, and become very happy.

CANARY BIRD.—If you dream that you hear a Canary sing, it denotes your marriage, and a comfortable habitation. It denotes that your partner will be cheerful and tender and very kind to you. If a married woman dreams she sees two canaries in a cage, it prognosticates twins.

CANDLES.—To dream that you are making candles, denotes that you will be very useful to others; if you dream that you are buying candles, it indicates feasting and rejoicing. To dream that you see a candle burning brightly, portends that you will receive a letter containing pleasing intelligence: but if you dream that you see a candle snuffed or blown out, it denotes the death of a friend or near relative,

CANNON.—To dream of hearing the firing of cannon, denotes national war, and personal trouble and vexation. To a young woman it denotes her future husband will have been a soldier.

CAPTIVE.—To dream of becoming a captive is a sign of insolvency, and imprisonment for debt. It is also a sign of an unhappy marriage, suffering from the bad disposition and misconduct of the wife or husband, as the case may be.

CAP.—To dream of a female with a fine cap is a sign that she is in love with you. But she would make a foolish wife. To dream you see a man with a cap on, denotes that your lover is a silly fellow, and will care but little for you after the honeymoon.

CART.—To dream of riding in a cart denotes that you will come down in the world, and have many hard changes. To dream of driving a cart indicates poverty and great straits.

CARVING.—To dream that you are carving meat for others denotes that you will be a benefactor; and to be carving meat for yourself denotes prosperity in your trade; if single, that you will succeed in love.

CARPET.—To dream that you are in a carpeted room denotes advancement to a state of riches.

CARRIAGE.—If you dream of riding in a carriage, it is a dream of contrary, and betokens a state of poverty.

CATS.—An unfavourable dream, denoting treachery and deceit. If a young woman dreams of cats it is a sign that her lover is sly and very deceitful; if a young man dreams of cats, she whom he loves will be a vixen, and will be sure to wear the breeches. If a tradesman dreams of cats, it denotes bad and dishonest servants. To dream of a cat and kittens is a sign of a numerous family, but not too good ; trifling and vain. To dream that you kill a cat is an omen that you will discover your enemies, and defeat their purposes.

CATTLE.—If you dream of cattle grazing in a pasture, it is a good sign of prosperty and affluence. If you dream of driving cattle it portends that if you are diligent and industrious, you will amass a great fortune. Black and large horned cattle denote numerous and violent enemies.

CATHEDRAL.—To dream that you are in a cathedral denotes that you will have a competency, to enable you to travel and see antiquities. To married persons, it denotes good children, some of whom will be eminent in the church.

CHAINS.—To dream you see chains is a token that enemies are concerting to harm you, but that you will escape their meshes. If you dream that you are confined in chains, it betokens very severe trials for a time, from which you will in time be extricated. To dream that a person puts a gold chain upon your neck indicates great favour ; and to the lover conjugal union and felicity.

CHAMBERMAID.—To a man, this intimates marriage with a high and arbitrary dame, and that he will have to knuckle under.

CHAFF.—This dream indicates that your schemes are not well-formed, and they will prove abortive ; and if you love, the person whom you love will

prove empty-headed, notwithstanding great preten-
sions and *bumpkum*.

CHEESE.—To dream of Cheese denotes deception
and infidelity in a lover. If the cheese be mity, it
denotes numerous little meddling persons who will
annoy you. To dream of eating cheese betokens
regret for having acted imprudently.

CHERRIES.—To dream of cherries in winter implies
disappointment in business, and in the marriage
state, and deceit in love.

CHILDREN.—If a married woman dreams of her
confinement, it denotes that she will soon be con-
valescent, and have a healthy child. If a single
woman dreams of having a child, her virtue will be
threatened.

CHICKENS.—To dream of a hen and chickens is
the forerunner of ill luck; your lover will desert
you, and marry another. To a farmer, it denotes a
bad season.

CHILDREN.—This is a lucky dream, and denotes
success in trade, and increase of wealth; to dream
that you see your child die, is a dream of contrary;
the child will recover.

CHURCH.—To dream that you go to church in
mourning, denotes a wedding; if you go in white, it
denotes a funeral.

CHURNING.—To dream that you are churning, is
a sign of prosperity and plenty. To the single, it
portends a happy marriage. To the farmer, a good
season and good crops, and to all it is an omen of
abundance and good health.

CLOCK.—To dream you hear the clock strike denotes a speedy marriage, and that you will be very comfortable in life. To dream that you are counting the hours, if in the forenoon, it indicates much happiness; but if in the afternoon, that misfortune and danger will attend you; that your false lover doats upon another. If the clock strikes roughly, and not the full hours, it denotes the failure of your health, and probably your death.

CLOUDS.—To dream of dark clouds suspended over you, it indicates that you will have to pass through great sorrows sufficient to overwhelm you. But if the clouds break, and roll away, your sorrows will pass away, and prosperity be your lot.

CLOTHES.—If you dream that you have plenty of clothes is a dream of contrary; you will want clothing. If you dream that you are naked, it is a sign that you will be well clothed. For a woman to dream that she is making children's clothes, is a sign of a particular state. If a sailor dreams that he has lost his clothes by shipwreck, it is a sign of marriage.

CLOVER.—"I do not know a better dream than this," says old Ptolemy. If you are in a field of clover, it is an omen that you will do well, be in health, and very happy. Art thou in love? Well shalt thou succeed. Thy wife shall be thy comfort always, and thy family shall prosper. To dream this, thou art highly favoured. If you are in love nothing can be more favourable, and all your undertakings will prosper and be advantageous to you. To the lover it also foretells that his intended wife will have great wealth and many children.

COFFEE.—This dream is favourable. It denotes settlement in life, prosperity, great happiness in the married state. To a single person it promises a faithful, affectionate, and confiding lover.

COFFIN.—It is a bad dream. It is a sign of the death of some dear friend; that death will rob the lover of the one so dear to him. As to the community, it is a sign of great mortality.

COLD.—This is a dream of contrary. It denotes comfort in your circumstances; kind and loving friends; you may have short trials, but you will happily surmount them.

COLLIERY AND COALS.—To dream that you are near a coalpit, denotes that you will be exposed to danger, and to dream that you are in a coalpit, is a sign that you cannot escape. Affliction is sure to follow dreaming of coals; losses in trade, and disappointment in love. To see coals burning bright and clear is favourable, the love of your intended is sincere. If you dream that the coals are extinguished, it foretells your own death, or that of a friend.

COLOURS.—Dreaming of colours, flags, and banners streaming in the air denotes elevation from obscurity, and that you will be highly honoured and esteemed.

COMBAT.—To dream of a combat with any one, denotes rivalry, and that you will seek revenge. If you dream that your combat ends in victory, it is a sign that you will retain the affections of your lover.

COMETS.—"I never dreamed of a comet," says old Ptolemy, "but it portended great calamity among the nations, as war, famine, and plague, and even cold-blooded murder. All persons, after such a dream may look for misfortune. It signifies descent from every situation to a lower. If you dream of a comet, do not travel, nor expose yourself where danger is, nor undertake any hazardous enterprise. If you do you will suffer."

COMMUNION.—To dream that you are partaking of bread and wine in church or chapel, is at all times favourable, it foretells many enjoyments. To the maiden it denotes virtuous love in him with whom she associates.

COMPANION.—To dream of your companion denotes abiding friendship.

CONCUBINE.—If you dream of speaking to a concubine, indicates that you sink into immorality, lose your character, and awfully suffer in consequence. It is a bad dream to you, very.

CONCERT.—To dream of a concert is a dream of contrary, denoting wrangling and disputation—disagreement among relations.

COOKING.—Dreaming of cooking denotes a convivial party, and also a wedding of some friend. It also denotes a family made happy by the abundance of this world's good.

CORKS.—To dream that you are corking bottles, indicates that soon you will have cause to make an entertainment on account of a favourable change in your circumstances. If you draw corks, it is a sign of the visit of some particular friend.

CORN-FIELD.—"To dream of cornfields, or corn," says Ptolemy, "is a most favourable omen. It betokens health, a happy family, a prosperous trade, great wealth. Thy speculations shall prosper. Art thou a tiller of the soil? Well shalt thou succeed. Dost thou ply the great deep in thy ships? Favourable breezes shall be thine, and large well-paying freights. Art thou a lover? Thy life shall be a perennial honey-moon. Well hast thou dreamed. Thine old age shall be green and happy. I congratulate thee on thy dream, whoever thou art!"

CORPSE.—To dream you see a corpse predicts a hasty, inconsiderate, and imprudent marriage, in which the parties will be very unhappy; they will be unequally yoked together. The children will be unhealthy, have bad dispositions, to make it a family of misery.

COW.—To dream that you are pursued by a cow, denotes an enemy; if you escape it, you will defeat your enemy. To dream of milking a cow is a sign of abundance. If a woman dreams of a cow calving, its a sign of a difficult confinement.

CRABS.—To dream of a crab denotes reverses, and to a sailor danger of shipwreck, and drowning.

CROWN.—To dream of a monarch's crown, denotes favour with the great, and elevation in your state. To dream that you wear a royal crown is a dream of contrary; it denotes your degradation. To dream that you give a crown, shows that you will rise to independance.

CROWS.—This is a sign of a funeral.

CRUCIFIX.—To dream of holding a crucifix indicates trials and crosses. If you hold it long, it denotes heroism in your future misfortunes.

CUCKOO.—This dream denotes temporary disappointments in love, even a rupture; but eventually you will secure by marriage the person whom you love. If you dream that you hear the cuckoo, and she stutters, it denotes that you will not succeed in business or love. To the married it is the omen of widowhood.

CUCUMBERS.—This is a dream of contrary. As cucumbers are deemed unwholesome, it denotes health; for the afflicted to dream of cucumbers, it denotes speedy restoration to health. To a single person, it denotes a happy engagement, and eventually an agreeable marriage.

DAIRY. — To dream that you are in a dairy, making butter, denotes that you will be very fortunate in your secular concerns; that you will marry a plain homely person, and be happy and have many children.

DARK.—If you dream that you are in darkness and cannot find your way, and you stumble, it denotes a change in your temporal affairs for the worse; by your imprudence, you will dreadfully commit yourself. But if you dream that you emerge from the darkness, and behold the sun, it denotes your ultimate escape; you will be happy, and regain your reputation.

DANCE.—This is a favourable dream; it indicates that you will be the recipient of great favour and honour; that your plans will succeed; that in love you will win the hand of a valuable person.

DEAD.—To dream of your relatives and friends who are dead, denotes personal or relative affliction, and also much mental suffering. If you dream that they are happy, it is a sign favourable to you.

DEATH.—This is a dream of contrary; it augurs happy long life. To the single it denotes an honourable and happy marriage. If a sick person dreams of death, it portends death.

DEER.—This is an unfavourable dream. It portends quarrels and dissensions in which you will be a party. If in trade it denotes embarrassment and failure, ending in imprisonment. It is a bad dream for the tradesman, the merchant, the sailor, and all official characters.

DESERT.—To dream that you are travelling across a desert, is a sign of a difficult and dangerous journey, especially if you dream that the weather is wet and boisterous. If you see the sun shine, your journey, and all affairs will be safe and prosperous.

DEVIL.—This is a shocking dream; and I fear that those who dream of him, are too much akin to him. It is high time for them to mend; for this dream portends great evil which the " father of lies" will bring upon them. It is better to pursue virtue, which is devil's bane.

DEVOTION.—To dream that you are devotional, and at your devotions is a good sign of bodily health, and temporal happiness.

DIAMOND.—This dream indicates solid and extensive wealth. Ptolemy says, " Dreaming of a diamond thou lover, thy wife will be a diamond to thee, very precious ; right happy shalt thou be. Man of commerce, if thou dreamest of diamonds great quantities of gold will roll into thy lap. Seamen and sailors, dream away about diamonds, for it betokens to you great good. Barren woman, dream of diamonds, and children thou shalt have, and good ones too."

DICE.—To dream that you are playing with dice, is a sign of great changes in your business and circumstances ; it betokens your life to be much chequered ; and your enterprises very hazardous.

Let the female look well to the private character of her lover. Is he a gambler? There lies her danger. To a young man, it denotes that he will lose the respect of those upon whom he is dependant.

DINNER.—If you dream that you are getting your dinner, it is a dream of contrary. It foretells straits and difficulties, and that you will often want a meal. You will not be comfortable in the married life. Your wife and children will be a source of pain to you.

DIRT.—To dream that your person or clothes are dirty, denotes sickness and sorrow. It also implies loss of virtue and reputation. To dream that one throws dirt upon you, is a sign that enemies will try to injure your character. Beware of some in whom you are so confiding.

DISASTER.—It is a dream of contrary; you will hear of the exaltation of some friend in whom you are interested, and it will lead to a marriage. What! if it be you? To dream of disasters at sea portends a prosperous voyage. It is a favourable dream for a man of business.

DISEASE.—To dream that you are diseased, it is a sign to a sick person of recovery; to the young man it is a warning against evil company, and intemperance. It is not a favourable dream for lovers. It denotes infidelity. If any have a law-suit, this dream is a bad omen.

DISPUTE.—Disputes always foretell quarrels and dissensions, and impediments to your success in trade; yet all will be of short continuance, you will surmount every trial. To a lover, to dream of disputes betoken some disagreement, which it will be difficult to make up.

DISTANCE.—To dream that you are at a distance from your friends, foretells family quarrels, and alienation. To dream of any friend at a distance, indicates that you will agreeably hear of them shortly.

DITCH.—To dream of ditches is unfavourable. It betokens great danger, great losses, great injuries, and many malignant enemies coming upon you. The lover who dreams that he or she falls into a ditch, is a sign that the contemplated marriage will be a bad one. For a tradesman to dream of falling into a ditch, it is a sign of bankruptcy.

DIVING-BELL.—To dream of a diving-bell is a happy omen; it indicates every kind of happiness—a brisk trade—a joyful family; and if in love, a successful consummation by marriage. You will be rich, virtuous, and honoured.

DIVORCE.—This is a dream of contrary. If a married person dreams of sueing for a divorce, it is a sign of the fidelity of his or her partner, and that he has no cause for jealousy.

DOLPHINS.—This is not a good dream. It indicates the death of some friend at sea; and the shipwreck of a vessel in which you are interested; the failure of the bright hopes of a lover; that your present prospects are futile; they will all be blasted; if you travel, it denotes great danger.

DOCKS.—To dream that you are standing by the docks in a sea-port town, denotes you will hear favourable news from abroad.

DOGS.—If you dream that a dog fondles with you, you will meet with faithful friends. But if he bites you, your best friend from some cause, will become your greatest enemy. If it only barks at you, you will quarrel with your friend or lover, and they will seek to injure you but in vain.

DOVES.—This is a fortunate dream. It denotes progressive prosperity in business; permanent esteem and affection of friends, peace in the family. If you love, your love will be warmly returned. If you hear the voice of a turtle-dove, it is an omen of the death of a dear friend. If you see in your dream a dove shot, and fall to the ground, it is a sign of your own death. To the lover it denotes that his love is returned with all the fervour he could desire, that he will marry and be very happy for many years, but that he will lose his wife and die a widower. It indicates the same to a young woman, with the exception that she will be left a widow at an early age.

DOWER.—If you dream of receiving a dower, it is a sign that the riches of your intended is nothing but a pretence to possess you. It is a dream of contrary.

DRAUGHTS.—To dream of playing at draughts is a sign that you have no fixity about you; that you are whimsical and given to change, and will never prosper till your loose course is altered. To dream of playing at draughts is not a good sign for any; it denotes poverty, unhappiness, and uncertainty, alternation of wealth and misery; that love too will alternate, first warm, hot, then cold.

DRESS.—To dream of buying a dress, denotes advancement; and that you will obtain your wishes. To dream of being well dressed is a sign of the approval of your friends and lover.

DRINK.—To dream that you are drinking at a fountain, is a sign of much happiness and enjoyment. If the water is muddy, it denotes approaching trouble. If you are thirsty, and cannot find water, it portends that your trials will have to be borne without any assistance. You will need self-reliance. To dream that you give drink to the thirsty foretells your sympathetic heart and your benefactions when required.

DRIVING.—If you dream of driving a gig, expect losses in trade. To dream that some one is driving you in a carriage is a good sign; it foretells a marriage. If you dream of driving any vehicle, it betokens your dependance, and poverty. To dream of driving an ass, is a sign that you will be tyrannical with your husband or wife, as the case may be.

DROPSY.—To dream of dropsy, denotes great bodily sickness, and aberration of mind, nearly insanity; it portends suicide by drowning, or casual drowning at sea. Let the dreamer be very careful and watchful.

DROWN.—To dream that you are drowning denotes overwhelming difficulties, losses in trade, and by death. If you dream you are drowning, and some one, or a life-boat, &c. rescues you, it is a sign that some friend will efficiently help you in your difficulties and sorrows.

DRUM.—To dream you hear the sound of a drum, with its musical accompaniments is a sign of national and family turmoils, and disorders, and that the country will be afflicted with war.

DRUNK.—To dream that you are drunk, denotes your fall into prodigality and ruin, and that you will be reckless of your substance, reputation, and domestic comfort. If a female dreams she sees a drunken man, it is a sign that her future husband will be intemperate.

DUCKS.—"I know that this dream is fortunate and unfortunate," says an ancient astrologer; "if you see the ducks flying, it is an omen of the increase of riches; if you see them swimming, on the glassy water; it is a good sign to the merchant, to the artizan, and to his family; and he or she who loves may calculate on falling into the lap of peace, and plenty. If you see them dive and bring up worms, it denotes a life of drudgery and servile dependance. To dream that you see a duck and a drake augurs that your wished for marriage will soon take place.

DUMB.—Dreaming of being dumb, portends that you will so demean yourself as to be devoid of all apology.

DUST.—To dream that you are almost blinded with dust, indicates the failure of your business, and the dispersion of your family. But if in your dream you get clear of it, you will recover your former state.

DWARF.—This is a dream of contrary. If you dream you see a dwarf, it is a sign that you will be elevated in rank. If you dream that you are a dwarf, it denotes health, muscular strength, and independent and commanding circumstances. To the tradesman, the farmer, and the lover, it is a lucky dream.

EARTHQUAKE.—This foretells much trouble to the dreamer: it indicates great losses in trade, bereavement; family ties death will dissolve; it also denotes family quarrels, the interruption of domestic happiness.

I fear too it is a sign of national calamities, commercial distress, and probably war. It augurs the dissolution of the lover's bond, and heart-breaking agony.

EARWIG.—An enemy! He will threaten to undermine the basis of your prosperity and happiness. He works very secretly.—A rival! a rival! Mind he does not covertly steal the heart of your lover.

EATING.—To dream that you are eating is an unfortunate omen, portending family quarrels, separations of lovers, losses in trade, bad harvest, and shipwrecks at sea. To dream that you sea other persons eating and you with them, denotes choice friendship, and eminent success in your trade or profession. In the conjugal state, you will be very happy, loving your wife, and be loved by her.

ECHO.—To dream you hear an echo to your own voice denotes that the letter you have sent will be met by a favourable answer, that the person to whom you have proposed will accept you; that your children will be beautiful and lovely, and good. Mind you do not idolize these little echoes! You will also hear of an absent friend.

ECLIPSE.—Old Ptolemy says this is a strange dream. "Man of ambition," says he, "hoping thy rich relation would leave thee a fortune; thy hope is eclipsed; for another has supplanted thee. Man of ease, expect to hear, according to thy dream of the death of thy parents, or other fraternity. Thou doatest on thy wife, or husband, or child, as the case may be; but death is coming; thy sun of happiness shall be eclipsed. Loving swain, gentle maiden, I know what ye like best,—marriage; it shall not be; ye dreamed of an eclipse; your hopes are darkened. Hope is fled. O confiding one, thy friend is a traitor and all thy expectations from him are obscured. A change, a change in every department of thy life—a reverse is prognosticated by thy dream of an eclipse! Learn wisdom therefore."

EDUCATION.—To dream of education in any way denotes your advance in literary fame. You will be much esteemed.

EGGS.—To dream of seeing a great number of eggs, indicates success in trade and in love. It also denotes a happy marriage and good children, and great prosperity. Do you hope for advancement to a better station, or office, it shall be yours. To dream that the eggs prove rotten denotes unfaithful and treacherous friends and lovers. To dream of eating eggs portends great enjoyment.

ELDERBERRIES.—To dream of this fruit portends sickness and death. It denotes a very uncertain courtship.

ELEPHANT.—To dream of an elephant denotes health, and strength; and that you will associate with the respectable of society.

ELOPEMENT.—To dream that you are eloping with your lover, indicates an unhappy marriage state; prognosticating much discomfort, if not misery. You will have a bad partner. That your spouse will be thoughtless and extravagant in all things, as well as hasty and quarrelsome in disposition. If you dream that your lover has eloped with some one else, the sooner you break that engagement the better; for your rival is likely to supplant you. To dream of a relative or friend eloping denotes their marriage, and unless you quickly come to some definite understanding, you will be supplanted. To dream of some friend or acquaintance eloping, is a sign of a sudden death.

EMBROIDERY.—To dream of embroidery, denotes deceit in those who apparently love you.

EMPLOY.—To dream that you want employment is a sign of prosperity. To dream that you have abundance of employment, denotes that you will have nothing to do. To dream that you employ others, is a sign that, if you are not mindful, you will injure them. This is a dream of contrary.

ENTERTAINMENT.—To dream of a place of entertainment, is the forerunner of some joyful festivity, where you will come in contact with your intended, and heart will meet heart. If you felt great pleasure in your dream, marriage will soon crown your wishes. If you felt unwilling to leave the entertainment, your marriage will be a very happy one. It is a good dream for the merchant, and tradesman. To the sailor it betokens a prosperous voyage, and a safe return, and to the soldier safety in battle.

ENVY.—To dream that you are envied is a sign that you will be admired and loved; and that if you have a rival, he will yet be utterly confounded. This is a dream of contrary.

EPICURE.—To dream that you see an epicure, portends that you will see a sick friend; if you dream that you are an epicure, it denotes your own sickness.

ERMINE.—To dream you see any one arrayed in this beautiful and expensive fur, portends that you will rise to great honour and dignity. If you dream that you are arrayed in ermine, it denotes a great and magnificent state awaiting you.

ESCAPE.—To dream that you try to escape from any danger, and cannot denotes continued trouble. To dream that you escape from sickness, from an enemy, from fire and water is a good sign; you must have trouble for a season; but eventually you will be delivered. If you escape from a serpent, depend upon it, it behoves you to enquire into the character of your lover. Is the party a snake in the grass? If so, escape for thy life.

EVERGREENS.—Lasting happiness! lasting love! lasting honour! perennial domestic bliss. Fresh engagements will be crowned with success. Speak to her! Speak to him, and the golden knot is tied. Enter the ship, cross the sea; safely shalt thou return. Go to new position, change thy residence; thou shalt be happy. Thy dream is of an Evergreen.

EXILE.—If you dream that you are banished, it implies that you will have to travel much.

FABLES.—If you dream that you are reading, telling, or hearing fables, it denotes that you will have agreeable friends, with whom you will have very agreeable association. To a lover it indicates that his or her intended is dissatisfied with you.

FACES.—If you dream that you see your own face in a glass, it is a sign that your secret plans will be discovered, and that you will fall into condemnation. If you see in dreaming many strange faces, it portends a change of your present abode, and associations. If you gaze in your dream upon the faces of friends, &c., it is a sign of a party, or wedding, to which you will be invited.

FAILURE.—To deam that you fail in business—

that you fail in securing the person that you love—
that your plans answer not,—is a dream of contrary;
it indicates that, by wise and cautious procedure, in
all things you will succeed.

FAIR.—It is very unlucky to dream of being at a
fair, it portends negligence in your business, and its
failure, and also false friends. The persons about
you are not so honest as they should be. Through
rivalry the lover is likely to suffer loss.

FAIRY.—"To dream that you see a fairy," says
Sergeius, the ancient astrologer, "is a very favourable
dream. Beggars have had this dream, and afterwards
become very rich. Swains and maidens have come
to me, and related this dream, and I have said,
Happy man! a noble wife for thee, and a rich
dowry too: happy woman! thou wilt find a husband
indeed. The first month of thy delicious enjoyment,
shall go through every month of every year, and
many years, of thy happy life! The labouring man,
the trader, who dreams this dream shall rapidly rise
into independence. And the bearing woman shall be
safely delivered."

FALCON.—This is a very bad dream. There is a
foe near you, full of envy, very near you, injuring
you with the tongue, and mind he or she does not
injure you with the hands. Art thou loving a person?
There is one intending to rob thee.

FALL.—To dream that you fall from an eminence,
from a tree, or the edge of a precipice, denotes a
loss of situation, and of property. If you are in love,
you bestow your attachments in vain; you will never
marry the person. To the tradesman, it denotes a
failing business, embarrassment, &c. To the sailor it
denotes a stormy voyage and shipwreck

FALSE.—" I never heard of any one dreaming that he met with false friends," says old Ptolemy, "but it indicated the very reverse; true, firm, and lasting friendship; a lover not of mushroom growth, but like an evergreen, always perennial !"

FAMINE.—This is a dream of contrary, denoting national prosperity, and individual comfort, in wealth and much enjoyment. You will have many friends, a true lover, and a happy family.

FARM.—To dream that you are taking a farm, denotes advancement. Probably some will bequeath property to you, and make you independent. If you dream of visiting a farm, and of partaking of its produce, it is a sign of good health. If you are single and unengaged, and a young person there serves you with something to eat and drink, you will soon be in love very agreeably. If a very old person is only seen, you may see in that old bachelorism or old maidism.

FARTHING.—To dream that you are not worth a farthing, or that some one gives you a farthing is a positive dream of evil. It portends a coming down in the world.

FAT.—" I once dreamed that I was getting fat," says old Quinsey, the astrologer, "and it was followed by a bad illness; and my wife Lucretia had the same dream, and she fell into a violent fever. My son, Ibeera, had a similar dream, and he had a fracas with his lover; they separated, and the false one wed another. Yea, this is a dream inspired by Sathanas, an intimation that the evil spirit meditates you ill."

FATHER.—To dream of your father, denotes that he loves you; if he be dead, it is a sign of affliction.

FAWN.—For a young man or young woman to dream of a young deer, is a sign of inconstancy. If a married woman has such a dream, it portends fruitfulness.

FEASTING.—This is an unfavourable dream, portending disappointments, enemies, and great lowness of spirit. Mind you are not thrown down on a bed of sickness. Ardent lover, dreaming of wedding thy dear one, this dreaming of feasting is bad for thee. A rival, even death ; will frustrate thy intentions.

FIDDLE.—This dream is a sign of prosperity, and of great enjoyment. You will receive joyful intelligence of a beloved distant friend. It is a sign that your lover will be accepted, and his suite will issue in happy wedlock—an agreeable companion, and good children. To the sailor it betokens a prosperous voyage, and return to the arms of his faithful lover. To dream that you are tuning and playing the fiddle, denotes your speedy marriage. If in your dream the strings break, you will never wed.

FIELDS.—To dream that you are walking in green fields, augurs very great prosperity, and agreeable circumstances, whether in trade or in love. To dream of being in withered or scorched fields, denotes coming poverty. To dream that you are in clover fields, or barley and wheat fields, and the crops are luxuriant, it denotes very great wealth, and agreeable connexions. If you dream that you are in a field newly ploughed and harrowed, denotes that success is before you ; but that you will have to make many sacrifices, and to be very indefatigable previously. If you are about a situation, be sure you will get it and be very comfortable. If you dream of being in a meadow or clover field, you will marry a rich and very handsome person, and will have many lovely children who will grow up very accomplished. Such a dream is a sure prognosticator of happiness in love and marriage, and great success in business and speculation. On the other hand, to dream of being in a ploughed field denotes great trouble, sorrow, and deprivation, and a very hard struggle through life for a decent livelihood.

FIGS.—This is a favourable dream, denoting that you are likely to receive a munificent gift which will raise you to comparative independance.

FIGHTING.—This dream certainly portends disagreements and quarrels in families. It also denotes misunderstandings among lovers, if not temporary separation. If you dream that a person fights you and beats you, it is a sign that the malice of your enemies will be successful; if you beat him, that you will defeat the malignant policy of your foes. It is a bad dream for the merchant, the soldier, and the sailor.

FILBERTS.—To dream of eating good ripe filberts indicates that a sick person will recover; and to a person in health it denotes the continuance of the same, and that he will live to an old age. It is a very favourable omen for the lover, portending the speedy nuptial ceremony. If you dream that the shell is empty, or that the kernel is worm-eaten, it is a bad omen—of false and disappointed hopes, and pretending friends. The lover will have to mourn over the false-hearted.

FIRE.—"Thou hast dreamed of fire, hast thou?" said Benevant, the great astrologer; "why, thou hast had a luck dream. It betokens for thee health and great happiness, kind relations, and warm friends. And if a young dame or hind, or lady and gentle-

man should thus dream, then that which you sigh
for, crave, and weep for, marriage, shall soon be
yours. Be patient a little! But if you dream that
you are burned with the fire; it portends calamity.

FISHING.—To dream that you are fishing and
obtain no fish, is an omen of bad success in business,
or in love. If you angle them, it augurs the acquisition of riches. If you see the fishes at the bottom
of the water, it being very clear, it is a sign of
wealth and grandeur.

FISH.—To dream of seeing a number of fishes of
a choice kind, and delicious to eat, indicates that
you will have much pleasure in all your engagements; you will be comparatively independent. If
you dream that a fish eludes your grasp, slipping
from your fingers; it betokens loss of situation, of
friends, and especially of a lover.

FLEAS.—To dream that you are annoyed by them
indicates harm from evil and malicious enemies;
trade will decrease; friends prove false, and lovers
deceitful.

FLOODS.—For seafaring persons, merchants, &c. to
dream of floods is a favourable dream, denoting successful trade, and a safe voyage, but to ordinary
persons, it denotes bad health, law-suits terminating
unfavourably; also very malignant enemies, proving
injurious. If you are a lover, your rival will, like a
flood, sweep away from your embrace the object of
your affections.

FLOWERS.—To dream that you are gathering
beautiful and fragrant flowers, it is an indication of
prosperity; you will be very fortunate in all you
undertake. If in your dream, you bind the flowers

into a bouquet, it portends your very agreeable marriage. If the bouquet gets loose, and the flowers appear to be scattered, your brightest prospects, and most sanguine hopes will be blasted. If you dream of withered flowers, it portends failing health, and approaching death.

FLYING.—To dream of flying denotes that you will escape many difficulties and dangers. It denotes success in trade and in love. Very likely you will have to travel. If you dream that you are trying to fly very high, it is an indication that you will aspire after a position which you will never reach, and for an office, for which you are not qualified.

FOG.—It denotes great uncertainty. You wish to be accepted as a lover. It is doubtful. You have applied to your friends for assistance. They will never give it. You are speculating in shares, policies, they may ruin you. You are hoping to recover your health. It is contingent. The dream is bad. If you dream that the fog clears away and the sun shines, your state will be happily reversed—uncertainty will banish.

FORTUNE.—It is a dream of contrary. If you dream that one has left you a fortune, it is a sign that he will not. If you dream that your friend has got a fortune, it is a sign of his coming poverty. It is a bad dream.

FOUNTAIN.—To dream you see a muddy fountain indicates trouble. To see a crystal overflowing fountain, denotes abundance, freedom from want. You will be highly respected and honoured. The person whom you love will love you, and your love will be permanent.

FOWLS.—To dream of fowls denotes moderate comfort in temporal things; but in love, it denotes you will meet with slander and rivalry. Be on your guard.

FOX.—If you dream of a fox, you have a sly, lurking enemy—a competitor in trade determined to undermine your interests; and in love a rival determined to displace you. If you are engaged in a law-suit, your counsel is playing two parts, and you will be cast in the end.

FRAUD.—If you charge some one with committing a fraud, you will discover that you have been robbed, and the person who has robbed you. To dream that you have committed a fraud is a dream of contrary, denoting the public appreciation of your character of integrity and honour. If a lover, you will discover the covert acts of your rival, and gain the victory.

FRIENDS.—Dreaming alarmingly of a distant friend, is a sign that sickness, or some evil has befallen that friend. If your dream of distant friends be calm and pleasing, expect good news soon. Your lover will soon return, whose visits will be agreeable, and end in matrimony. Dreaming you see distant friends rejoicing, denotes prosperity to them and to yourself. If they weep the dream is bad. To dream you see a friend dead is a sign of marriage, and *vice versa*.

FRIGHTENED.—To dream that you are terrified at some object, or through any other cause, is a dream of contrary. Terror implies bliss; fright, joy; pain, pleasure. Your bargains, contracts, &c. will be successful. If you dream that you overcome your fears, there will be a glorious turn in your affairs, and you will swim on the tide of prosperity. And, O thou restless lover, all thy fears will be turned into pleasures. It shows that your engagement will end satisfactorily, only persevere and be not daunted by present appearances, however unfavourable they may seem.

FROGS.—Frogs are harmless creatures. To dream of them is favourable; it denotes success in business; to the farmer propitious season, and good crops, and healthy profitable cattle. To all classes, to young and old, it is a good dream, denoting good friends, and public patronage and support. To the lover it is a happy portent :—

> He or she who dreams of frogs,
>   Most certainly shall find,
> Maiden sweet, or swain most dear,
>   Each suited to the mind :
> A wedding gay is coming soon,
> Then, O then, for the honey-moon.

FROST.—This dream denotes very severe trials and troubles. If a female dreams it she is in danger of conquest through a deceitful sensual man, who will eventually desert her. To the man of commerce, it indicates great difficulties in trade.

FRUIT.—To dream of fruit has a different interpretation according to what the fruit is that you dream of. But to dream of a collection of numerous and varied fruits, both English and Foreign, portends unbounded acquisition of wealth—and an agreeable and wealthy matrimonial alliance—a numerous and happy family. The different fruits have different prognostications, thus :

Almonds foretell difficulties, loss of liberty, and deceit in love; bad weather to the sailor, and want of success to the tradesman.

Apples betoken long life and success, a boy to a woman with child, faithfulness in your sweetheart, and riches by trade.

Apricots denote health and prosperity, a speedy marriage, dutiful children, and success in love.

Cherries indicate disappointment in love, vexation in the married state, and slight in love.

Currants prefigure happiness in life, success in undertakings, constancy in your sweetheart, handsome children to the married, and riches to the farmer and tradesman.

Elderberries augur content and riches; to a maiden they bespeak a speedy marriage; to a married woman, that she will shortly be with child; to the tradesman success in business; to the farmer, good crops.

Figs are the forerunners of prosperity and happiness; to the lover they denote the accomplishment of your wishes; to the tradesman increase of trade; they are also indicative of a legacy.

Filberts forbode much trouble and anger from friends; to the tradesman they denote a prison, and decay of trade; to the lover a complete disappointment; to the married, care and undutiful children.

Gooseberries indicate many children, chiefly sons, and an accomplishment of your present pursuits; to the sailor they declare dangers in his next voyage; to the maiden a roving husband; and to the man a rakish wife.

Grapes foretell to the maiden that her husband will be a cheerful companion, and a great songster; they denote much happiness in marriage, and success in trade; if you are in love, they augur a speedy union between you and your sweetheart.

Lemons denote contentions in your family and uneasiness on account of children; they announce the death of some relation, and disappointment in love.

Medlars are a very good omen, they bespeak riches to the dreamer; that you will overcome your enemies, and if you have a lawsuit, you will surely gain it; to the lover they foretell a good husband or wife, with beautiful children and much happiness.

Melons announce speedy recovery to those who are sick; they are indicative of harmony, and inform you that you will speedily accommodate a dispute between you and others; in love, they announce constancy; and in marriage a partner of a happy temper, with handsome children.

Mulberries are of good import; to the maiden they foretell a speedy and happy marriage; to the lover constancy and affection in his mistress; they also denote wealth, honours, and many children; they are particularly favourable to sailors and farmers.

Nuts, if you see clusters of them, denote riches and happiness; to the lover success and a good-tempered sweetheart; if you are gathering of them, it is not a good omen, for you will pursue some matter that will not turn out to your advantage; if you crack them, the person who courts you, or to whom you pay your addresses, will treat you with indifference, and be very unfaithful.

Oranges are very bad omens; they forbode loss of goods and reputation, attacks from thieves, wounds and sickness in the object of your affections.

Peaches are very favourable to the dreamer; if you are in love, they foretell that your love is returned, that you will marry, have many fine children, and be very happy; they denote riches to the tradesman, good crops to the farmer, and a prosperous voyage to the sailor.

GALA.—To dream that you are at a fête or gala, indicates that you will be so circumstanced in life as to be able to enjoy yourself in travel to distant places. If you dream your lover is with you, it portends great conjugal happiness.

GALLOWS.—"This is a very strange dream," says the ancient philosopher, Philater. "It is a dream of contrary. I have known persons come to me and tell this dream to whom I have always said, you will be lucky in all ways; much trade—much money—much honour, a high position. And to the lover I have said, Wishes consummated — hearts tied fast — hands united — happy wedlock — blessed children! Happy lover!"

GAME.—To dream that you are playing at a game, and win, is a sign that you will be very unsuccessful. But if in your dream you appear to lose, it denotes you will be prosperous. If you love one, you will obtain that person as your partner for life.

GAME.—If you see game in the woods, and shoot it, it is a sign that you will obtain the heart you covet. If you dream of abundance of dead game, it denotes a marriage. If the game is decomposing, it denotes the decay of health, and trade. You will be disappointed in love.

GARDEN.—This is a very fortunate dream. Old Ptolemy calls it one of the best. Franximus says,

"I have interpreted many dreams; this among the rest; and have always proved it to be really good. After it I have seen persons rise and become independent of leaky friends—I have seen merchants successful, sailors have a pleasant voyage, farmers have weighty crops, and lovers crowning themselves with rosebuds. All who dream this must rise to wealth and honour." But observe the dream must be of a garden full of shrubs, flowers, and fruit.

GARTER.—To dream that you lose your garter denotes that your circumstance in life will be adverse and uncomfortable. If you dream that your lover picks it up, and gives it you, it denotes the sincerity of purpose, and strength of affection; if your lover gives it you not, you will find that lover a deceiver; should you be united, woe unto you!

GATHER.—To dream of gathering up money is a sign that your state will greatly improve. To gather fruit in season denotes great enjoyment, health, and happiness; but if out of season, it is grief without reason. It betokens enemies, and deceitful love. To dream you gather flowers, denotes that you will marry early and well, and that children, like olive-plants, will be round about your table.

GHOST.—To dream you see a ghost, and the sight appals you, is a very bad omen. Difficulties will come upon you of an overwhelming character. Malignant enemies will try to injure you. But if you are bold in your dream, and see the ghost vanish, it denotes that you will overcome all.

GIANT.—"There is a great difficulty to be encountered, if you have this dream," says Zanchius. "But meet it with pluck and decidedness of soul, and it will vanish. There again, thou dreamest of a giant; well, it means a knave of an enemy whom thou must encounter.   Beware of his dexterous baits — meet him fairly in the face—confront him boldly, and thy giant foe will skulk into *Lethe*."

GLASS.—To dream that you look clearly through glass, denotes the successful, and even tenor of your way.   If it is dim and not transparent, it denotes that your affairs, and your prospects, are very uncertain ; you will be in straits and difficulties.   If you dream you cannot see at all through the glass, your state will be decided.   " It denotes," says Fravellus, " when a lover sees obscure glass, a mutable lover, and an inconstant friend.   I never knew much luck come after this dream, and I have interpreted multitudes."

GLOVES.—To dream that you lose your gloves denotes loss in business, and loss in trade, a change of abode awaits you ; if you dream that you lose your right hand glove, if married, you will lose your partner ; if single, another will deprive you of your lover.

GOATS.—You will have enemies, and many trials through deceit ; but your mind will be happy under all ; your trials will not sink you, but operate for your good.   And you had better be happy in adversity than miserable in luxury and splendour.

GOD.—This is a dream which seldom occurs ; it is principally confined to those who are afflicted, and those about to die.   It is always a token of death ; except in conversation, when it denotes the prospect of obtaining mercy, and elevation to usefulness and honour.   To the pious it denotes a happy death.

GOLD.—" To dream of gold," says Ptolemy, " is a dream of contrary.   It is a sign of poverty and distress. Let the tradesman, the merchant, and the adventurer be careful how they place their capital; their speculations will be hazardous. Beware of speculations; it is not all gold that glitters. So with regard to love. To dream that thy lover has plenty of gold, denotes disagreement, when thou marriest thy lover. I fear it will be a sorry wedding. Gold is often an omen of sickness, sorrow, as the results of bad fortune."

GOOSE.—This is a bad dream, for a single man. The woman whom he loves will prove a very silly incompetent wife; she will be a regular gossip, never at peace with her neighbours, and always censuring and quarreling with her husband and his relations. He had better surrender her to some one else.

GOOSEBERRIES.—See *Fruit.*

GRAIN.—To dream that you see a quantity of grain is a most fortunate omen, it implies that by industry and perseverance you will become wealthy and be greatly respected and honoured. To the farmer it denotes favourable seasons, and good crops. If you are in love you will secure the heart of your lover, and have a numerous and happy family.

GRAPES.—See *Fruit.*

GRASS.—To dream that you see green grass, it is an omen that denotes great and continued prosperity; if you dream of withered and decayed grass, the dream is a sign of sickness and distress, and probably an indication to one whom you love.

GRAVE.—To dream of an opened grave is a sign of the dissolution of some near friend or relative. If you dream it under a severe illness, your recovery is doubtful.

GUN.—To dream that you hear the report of a gun, forbodes that you will hear of the death of a distant friend or relative; it also portends that you will be slandered very much by your enemies. But like the report of a gun, that opposition will soon pass away. If the lover dreams of hearing a gun, it denotes a rival determined to supplant you, or to revenge you. It also denotes bad luck to a trades-man, he will have losses through fraudulent debtors.

HAIL.—To dream that it is hailing or snowing, is a bad dream. It denotes disappointed hopes, and blighted prospects. To the farmer unpropitious sea-sons, and poor crops. To the lover unsuccessful ap-plication. To persons in trade heavy losses. Even friends will disappoint your expectations. Are your hopes fixed on your children? Alas! they will not realize those hopes.

HAIR.—If you dream that you have luxuriant hair, it denotes continued health and prosperity. If you dream that your hair is falling off, to a man it is the portent of bad trade; to the husband the omen of an afflicted wife, and vice versa; to the lover the death of his intended. If you dream that your hair turns gray, it is a sign of failing health, of a decaying business, and the decline of a lover's affection.

HAMMER.—To dream that you hear the sound of a hammer, denotes a brisk trade, and great gain. To the operative it is a sign of full employment, and good wages, and of good health, to enjoy the same. To a maiden it prognosticates an agreeable husband, who will ever be industrious, frugal, temperate, and decided to make her life happy, very likely too he

ING.—To dream that you are being hung,
denotes good to you. You will rise in society, be
patronised and wealthy. To dream that you see a
person hanged, is an omen of good to him. He also
will attain wealth, and great honour.

HARES.—To dream that you see a hare pursued
by dogs, is not a good sign; it portends enemies;
but you will be able to escape. To dream you see
a few hares, denotes choice and faithful friends. If a
hare runs towards you, it denotes the visit of a dear
friend. To a swain or maiden, it is the portent of
an early and happy marriage.

HARMONY.—To dream that you hear musical sounds floating in the air, or that you listen to harmony of any kind, is the portent of a long and happy life. In love it denotes that your lover is most amiable and affectionate, and sincerely attached to you. Marriage to you will be a happy boon. This dream is a good omen for all classes.

HARVEST.—To dream of harvest time, and that you see the reapers in the corn field reaping the corn and binding it in sheaves, or that you see the jocund reapers, and hear them shouting, "Harvest home!" is a most favourable dream. You could not have had a better. It denotes prosperity to the farmer especially, many customers for the tradesman, a safe and prosperous voyage to the mariner, and lucrative bargains to the merchant. If a lover dreams of harvest, it prognosticates the consummation of his or her wishes, in early wedlock, happy society, and a numerous and happy offspring.

HAT.—To dream you have a new hat portends success in any scheme. To dream that you lose your hat, or that another takes it off your head, you have an enemy not far off who will both openly and secretly seek your injury. To dream some one puts your hat on his head, it foreshows a rival; he will supplant you, or it denotes that some one is possessing property which certainly belongs to you.

HEAVEN.—To dream of heaven denotes a change of worlds, and that if you regard your dream, the remnant of your life will be spiritually happy, and your death peaceful. Do not forget this significant dream.

HEDGES.—To dream of green hedges is a sign of agreeable circumstances. If the hedges are flowery, it betokens great prosperity, and success in love. If you cannot pass on your way for thorny briery hedges, it denotes that in business, you will suffer by competitions, and in love, by determined and malignant rivals.

HELL.—This dream forbodes bodily suffering and mental agony, arising from restless enemies, loss in trade, bereavements, &c.

HERBS.—Different herbs are portentous according to their different natures, and medical virtues. Hemlock, Henbane, Aconite, and any poisonous herb, denotes you are surrounded with dangers. To dream of useful and fragrant herbs is good; it denotes agreeable circumstances. Sage denotes honour and advancement, the result of wisdom and prudence. Thyme portends to the lover a happy marriage, and to others, prosperity. Balm denotes sickness, but sure recovery; Horehound a chronic and incurable disease; Wormwood, bitter trials, and overwhelming disappointments. It is bad for the lover. To dream you are gathering herbs, and they are scarce, is a bad omen; if they abound, and are fragrant, it is a very good dream.

HERMIT.—If you dream that you have become a hermit and retired from the world, it indicates that you will have failures in trade, be reduced in your circumstances, and experience great mental depression, but that eventually you will rouse yourself, and surmount every conflict and difficulty, and become wealthy; but to the young it denotes that their marriage is an uncertainty.

HILLS.—To dream of ascending a high steep hill and you are unable to arrive at the top, it is a sign that you will have to labour and toil all your life, and have many difficulties and troubles, and will never be wealthy. It denotes that the lover will never marry, though he or she may approximate to it; something will occur to prevent matrimony. There is many a slip between the cup and the lip.

HOME.—To dream of the home of your childhood, and the scenes of your action in it, in company with your former play-fellows, indicates your continued health and prosperity. To the lover it betokens a true and responsive love, a happy marriage, and great conjugal happiness. You will have a numerous progeny, and each child will do well. To the husbandman, it is a good sign.

HOMICIDE.—To dream of committing this dreadful crime, is an evil dream, it portends many severe misfortunes and heavy losses. "I have frequently seen," says Etius Flaccius," most direful accidents follow this dream, robbery, fire, and death. Art thou a lover? Death will deprive thee of thy object. Art thou a merchant? Loss, loss, will be thine. Dost thou till the ground? Failing crops, diseased cattle, will be thy portion. O man, or, O woman, thy dream is bad indeed, you will be stained by some dreadful crime, and not escape law's penalty. O mother, thy embryo child will be a bad one, overbearing, dishonest, profligate, tyrannical, and degraded."

HONEY.—To dream you are eating honey denotes good health, long life, prosperity and great enjoyment. Your business will be all you can wish, lucrative, raising you to independance. It denotes that your lover is virtuous, sincere, and very fond of you. It would be death to part from you. It denotes that the husband, or the wife, will be of a sweet disposition, industrious, frugal, affectionate and faithful. In fact, as Ptolemy says, " It is a notable dream, foretelling sweetness in wedlock, in the domestic and social circle, and sweetness in all secular pursuits."

HORN.—To dream you hear the sound of a horn denotes intelligence from an absent friend in a distant country, though not of an agreeable nature. If you hear the sound repeatedly, it is a sign of disagreements, and even of war.

HORSE. — Dreaming of this noble animal is generally good. To dream that you are riding a handsome and good horse betokens future independance and happiness. But if it throws you, it denotes that your purposes will be thwarted. If you dream that horsemen approach you, it foretells that you will receive news from a distant friend. To dream of white horses, denotes a marriage, yours, if you are riding upon it. A black horse denotes death.

HOUNDS.—To dream of following the hounds indicates that your pursuits will not be very productive —that your conjugal affiance will disappoint you.

HOUSE.—To dream you build a house, foretells prosperity and success in trade. After such a dream, you may expect a great increase, with better profits. If a sailor dreams of building a house, it foretells a prosperous voyage, and that on his return, he will marry a wealthy woman, and will not go to sea again, except for pleasure.

HUMMING BIRDS.—This dream denotes travel to a foreign clime, and great success in business, or profession there. If you dream of a large flock of humming-birds, it foretells that you will be very fortunate and save money; if you see one dead, you will not succeed, but return to your own country.

HUNTING.—To dream that you hunt a stag, and capture it, is a right good sign of secular prosperity —to the lover, a sign that he will obtain his wish. To dream of hunting a hare denotes misfortune and trouble, and especially disappointment in love. To dream that you are hunting a fox, denotes wily competitors or rivals; if you kill him, it portends your triumph after severe contention.

HUNGER.—To dream that you are very hungry denotes that by your genius and industry you will rise in the world to wealth and honour; to the lover, that your sweetheart will undertake a journey before you marry; in business, prosperity.

HURRICANE.—"This dream I hate," says Tinea Ballater, the Arabian dream explainer, "for it always foreshadows evil. Danger to the traveller and sailor, and disappointment to the dearest lovers. It augurs ill for the trader, and the merchant, and it is the precursor of family feuds and quarrels."

HURT.—To dream of having hurt yourself, or that some one has hurt you, is a dream of contrary, implies that your projects will succeed whether as a lover or a person in business; and that all the malicious attempts of your enemies will prove abortive.

HUSBAND.—To dream you have one, is a dream of contrary; your wish will not be granted. To dream you fall in love with another woman's husband, indicates loose desires, and disregard to virtue. But for a widow to dream that she has a husband, and that he smiles upon her, indicates that she will soon have an offer, and it will be accepted.

HUSBANDRY.—To dream of the implements of husbandry, has a variety of interpretations. To dream of a plough denotes success in life, and a good marriage. To dream of a yoke is unfavourable, unless it be broken, — then it denotes a rising above your present condition. To dream of a scythe shows injury from enemies, and disappointment in love. To dream of a team, denotes death in the family of the dreamer; a sweetheart of very bad temper, and want of success in your undertakings.

HYMEN.—To dream of the god of matrimony, foretells speedy marriage with the person whom you love, and that the union will be very happy and be productive of a numerous family of boys and girls who will rise to eminence, and will do well in the world, and marry rich persons from some distant place.

HYMNS.—To dream of singing hymns indicates a devotional spirit, predicting much happiness, prosperity, and success to the dreamer. The lover will be fortunate, your loved one will be everything that could be desired, and very affectionate.

ICE.—Dreaming of ice is always bad. It foretells failure in trade, unsuccessful speculation and enterprise. It indicates that your now ardent lover is about to cool down and jilt you. To the sailor, it denotes disasters at sea. It is a bad dream for the farmer auguring devastation of crops.

ICICLES.—If you dream you see icicles suspended betokens good luck. If a man he will shortly marry a virgin of great beauty and accomplishments, who will be very much attached to him. They will have a large family of girls, who will have their mother's beauty and marry rich men. To a young woman it predicts a marriage with a man of wealth, and they will have a large family of boys, who will rise to eminence.

IDIOT.—This is a dream of contrary. It indicates that you transact business, and have friendships that you will receive advantages from, or marry an intelligent person. To dream that you are an idiot, foretells your competency for every future engagement.

ILL.—To dream that you are labouring under any illness, denotes that you are in danger of falling into a great temptation, which, if you do not resist, will injure your character. If you are not circumspect, your rival will supplant you.

ILLUMINATION.—Dreaming of an illumination, denotes some joyful occasion at hand. It generally denotes good fortune. In love, you will obtain your wish. In wedlock it is the omen of successful childbirth. Have you no lover? One is coming. Are you about to travel? You will travel successfully. Are you speculating? The prize is yours. Have you a law-suit? The decision will be in your favour. "This is a happy dream," says M. Bonar, "and I have always seen it followed by good."

IMPS.—This dream betokens great grief and vexation. The persons around you will very much annoy you. It indicates false and malicious, and revengeful persons, as your debtors or creditors, as the case may be. The lover is treading on dangerous ground, and trusting in a broken reed; and if he or she continues to trust it may lead to a broken heart.

IMPRISONMENT. — "It is a dream of contrary," says Dr. Sibly. "It prognosticates liberty in every sense, free enjoyment in all states, especially in wedlock."

INFANCY.—If a married woman dreams of infancy, it indicates a peculiar state. To dream of your own infancy, denotes good fortune in trade or profession, or in courtship and matrimonial affairs. To dream you are an infant again is bad.

INDIGENCE.—To dream that you are in indigent circumstances is a good omen, it denotes the receipt of a large sum of money, and is generally the forerunner of a fortunate occurance. If a woman *enceinte* dreams of being in poverty it foretells she will have a son who will become a great man, marry a foreign lady, and become very rich.

INFIRMARY.—To dream that you are in an infirmary, denotes an accident or sickness. To dream you leave it, is a sign of recovery. To dream that you are visiting the patients there foreshows an elevation in your position, and a feeling and generous heart.

INJURY.—To dream that some person or persons have injured you, denotes enemies who have evil designs against you. Beware of them. Walk circumspectly, and they will not succeed, though they will expose their malicious purposes. If a tradesman, your competitors will conspire against you, and you may sustain losses. To the farmer, such a dream predicts failure of crops by unpropitious seasons of fire. If you are a lover, then the friends of your intended are against you. Take care; you are so surrounded by foes and difficulties that a change of locality is desirable.

INK.—To dream that you are using ink denotes prosperity in business; if you spill it, and dirty your hands, it denotes that your correspondence will not be successful, whether in trade, or in love. You must expect an unfavourable answer.

INN.—It is unlucky to dream of being at an Inn, it denotes poverty and want of success in yonr undertakings; it is the forerunner of sickness, and sometimes death; it sometimes portends poverty, and imprisonment. To the tradesman it denotes loss of money, and a falling off in business. If you are in love, it portends that your sweetheart will jilt you and marry another.

INSANE.—"I have known very sensible and rational men," says Dr. Sibly, "dream that they were insane, and it has always proved a good dream, followed by good health, domestic happiness, rare social enjoyment, and long life. As to the lover, it shows extraordinary affection, decision of purpose, and entire consecration to the person loved."

INSTRUCTION.—To dream that you are receiving instruction, prognosticates that you will shortly be placed in circumstances as to need the advice and assistance of your friends, and it will be well if they come to your relief. To the lover, it indicates a dangerous rival, under which rivalry, you will need help and consolation. Let not jealousy foster revenge. To dream that you give instruction, denotes that your friends will be placed in a similar state, and will require your counsel and aid.

INSULT.—To dream that a person insults you, denotes that you will lose your lover through a silly and trifling quarrel. It also portends that what occurs will go in opposition to your wishes and interests, and that you will be very unfortunate for some time after your dream, unless you rouse yourself, and change your place of residence.

INTEMPERANCE.—To dream of being intemperate in either eating or drinking, foretells sickness and trouble. If a female dreams she sees a drunken man, it is a sign that her husband or lover, is defective in principle, and it will be well for her to renounce him. For a man to dream of an intemperate female, it predicts that his future wife will be a slattern, improvident, and probably drunken. If you see the intemperate party weeping, it denotes permanent virtue and happiness in association.

ISLAND.—To dream that you are on a desolate island implies the death of your lover. If it appears a fertile island, covered with vegetation it implies that your present lover will prove unfaithful; but you will soon meet with a more favourable match.

ITCH.—To dream of having the itch is an unlucky dream, denoting much difficulty and trouble in business and love, you will marry a person of irritable and restless disposition, you are likely to be in adverse circumstances, and very unhappy.

IVORY.—M. Dupone, the French astrologer, says. "This is a superior dream; to the lover it portends beauty, sweetness, virtue, and rare enjoyment. A young female told me this dream; she was poor; but I soon saw her riding in her own coach, with a smart rich man, as her husband. This dream portends abundance to the farmer, success to the merchant, and a safe and prosperous voyage to the sailor.

> Delighted may the maiden be,
> Whene'er she dreams of ivory;
> A rare good sign 'tis sure to prove
> Of fathful and abiding love,
> With one well-suited to her mind,
> A husband tender, loving, kind;
> Rich in estate, they will be one,
> Loving at first they will love on;

> The marriage-bond be crown'd with joys,
> And round their table girls and boys;—
> Yea, all this bliss is sure to be
> To those who dream of ivory!

IVY.—To dream of ivy is a sign that your friend, your lover, your husband, or wife, will adhere to you as ivy clings to the wall. You will have good health and live long. Your enemies will be powerless; you may smile at them defiantly. In trade, your customers will be constant and abiding. Happy maiden! Happy swain! true love is for you. You will be blessed in your house and store. To the husbandman, it foretells good and lucrative produce, and to sea-faring men, a safe and profitable voyage.

JACKAL.—This dream indicates that you have an inveterate, deep, and sly enemy who will leave no stone unturned to do you an injury, but much to his grief and vexation it will turn out for your advantage. While he falls you will rise; while he is disappointed, you will triumph. The crafty will be taken in their own snares. To dream that a jackal bites you, it implies you will be much annoyed by a rival who will triumph over your undecided lover. But your loss will turn out a happy one; though you may grieve at first.

JAIL.—To dream that you are in jail is a dream of contrary. Prosperity in business, freedom from embarrassment, and domestic happiness will be your lot. Quineas Philatus says, that if a virgin dreams that her lover is in jail, it is a sign that she has found an abiding lodgement in the heart of her lover, and will rest there till death do them separate. If a young man dreams that he is in jail, it is a sign that he will succeed in life, and marry the lady of his choice, the loss of whom he has had reason to fear. He will ever live as the idol of her heart. This is also a good dream for a widow. To dream of escaping from jail, denotes to the person in distress, a favourable change in his circumstances. The day of adversity will depart. It also indicates the recovery of health.

JAUNDICE.—To dream that you have the jaundice, is a bad dream, sickness, or poverty, or disagreements are at hand. If you dream, that your lover has got the jaundice, it indicates that he or she will soon discover their real character, which will cause them to sink in your estimation. Mere pretenders, hollow-hearted you will find them. To dream that your wife or husband has the jaundice, is not a good sign of their fidelity to you.

JACKDAW.—To dream that one crosses your path is a sign of bitter enemies, who will endeavour to blast your reputation, and injure you in your affairs. To dream that you catch a jackdaw is a sign that you will be able to defy them while they can do you no harm. It is not a good dream for persons, in religious society; it indicates opposition from some of their own sect. It is not a good dream for a farmer; it denotes indifferent crops.

JEALOUSY.—To dream that you are jealous of your husband or wife, or sweetheart, as the case may be, is indicative of trouble and great anxiety. If you are in business, you may expect your affairs to be very much agitated and interrupted from unforeseen causes, you will also experience many disappointments in money affairs, and trouble and annoyance on account of the failure of some with whom you do business, and also on account of

returned bills. To dream that another is jealous of
you, expect misunderstandings, distrust and altered
affection. But do not despair it will be all the
better for you.

JEWELS.—It is always a good dream, the harbinger of great prosperity, and a great amount of
wealth. To dream your lover gives you jewels, it is
a sign that his affection is real, and that he will
certainly marry you. If a young man dreams that
he sees his loved one adorned with jewels, and that
he is ravished with the scene, it foretells his speedy
and happy union ; that his bride will possess a sweet
and lovely disposition. To dream that both you and
your lover are counting and inspecting jewels, denotes a numerous and healthy, and fortunate offspring. This dream is good for the merchant, the
sailor, and the farmer.

JEWS.—It is a good dream to dream of a Jew, or
Jews. It denotes the accumulation of wealth. To a
lover, it denotes a speedy and fortunate marriage. It
also denotes travel to foreign countries, and successful enterprise there.

JOURNEY.—If you dream that you have to go a
journey to some distant country, foretells a great
change in your circumstances. If the journey is
pleasant such will be the change in your circumstances. If rough, and unpleasant, it is an unfavourable sign.

JOY.—This dream is a sign of good health, and
that you will receive a sum of money, or become
rich through the inheritance of an unexpected legacy
from a distant relative.

JUDGE.—To dream that you stand before a Judge,

indicates that you will be involved in some dispute, or have some serious charges made against you. It is a dream of contrary; for if you dream that the Judge acquits you, it indicates your discomfiture; if he condemns you, it augurs that your plea will be successful, and you will triumph over your enemies.

JUMPING.—To dream that you jump, augurs that you will meet with many impediments and trials; but by industry, courage, and perseverance, you will eventually surmount them. If a single person, it also implies that you will have a sweetheart much attached to you, but whose parents will oppose your union.

KEEPSAKE.—To dream that a friend or lover gives you a keepsake, it implies that some unexpected good will soon be possessed by you; that your friends are anxious for your welfare, and will do all they can to promote it. To a young man it denotes that his future wife will be rich in virtue, and beautiful in person, and will ever be affectionate and constant. To a young woman, it portends that your future husband will be gentlemanly, rich, and renowned, you will have many children, the pledges of your mutual love. To dream that you give keepsakes to others implies your future ability to do so, and you will move in circles of amiable and agreeable friends. But if a keepsake is asked of you, and you are unable to give it, it betokens further poverty and embarrassment, and much sickness.

KERNEL.—To dream of a good kernel, portends favourable circumstances. To dream of an unsound rotten kernel denotes that you will discover a false friend.

KEY.—To dream that you lose a key, denotes disappointment and displeasure. To dream you give a
key denotes a marriage ; to find or receive one, the
birth of a child ; to dream of many keys, denotes
riches, as the result of a flourishing trade.

KILL.—To dream you see a person killing any
fowl, bird, or animal, portends that your lover will
place his affections on another, and will desert you.
To a married woman it announces that some false
friend of her husband will make improper advances
to her.

KING.—To dream of being in the presence of mon-
archy, and that you speak to a sovereign, indicates
that you will rise to honour and dignity in your
country. If the monarch is unfriendly, the dream is
unfavourable, and all your expectations will be
blasted. If a maiden dreams that she is in company
with a king, it foretells that her future husband will
be well off, and probably occupy a situation under
government.

KISS.—To dream of kissing one whom you should
not, is a bad sign ; it denotes a false friend, or a false
lover. To see another kiss your intended, portends a
rival. To see your lover kiss another person, denotes
false love from a false heart. To dream that your
lover kisses you with affection, and repeatedly, shows
that lover to be true to you, and that his intentions
are pure. For married persons to dream of kissing
each other, portends that you will meet with an unfaithful companion.

KITE.—To dream you see a kite flying high, portends elevation in your station in life. If you are
flying it yourself successfully, and if it flies high and

steadily, it is a good sign. You are sure to rise above your present position to dignity and honour; some high official station will be yours. In love it is a good dream, especially for a widow. It frequently foretells travel in distant countries. The farmer may expect large crops,—the sailor a safe and prosperous voyage, and commercial men, a good trade. But if the string should break, and the kite be blown away, it is as bad a dream as you can have. All your enchanting prospects will be blasted.

KITTEN.—To dream that you are playing with a kitten, and that it scratches or bites you, denotes that your sweetheart has a trifling mind, and is of a spiteful disposition, and that if you marry you will have a very unhappy life, and wish yourself single again.

KNAVE (*at cards.*)—To dream of playing at cards, and that you continually hold the knave of diamonds in your hand portends seduction. The knave of hearts, you will meet with a lover; the knave of spades early widowhood and the knave of clubs debt and imprisonment.

KNIFE.—This is a very unfavourable dream. If you see knives cleaned ready for a feast, it is by contrary sign, a portent of poverty. If you see them bright and sharp, it denotes your enemies, and their evil designs against you. If you have a lawsuit pending, it is sure to terminate against you. If you are married, your partner will prove false to you; and if you are a lover, the loved one will reject you and marry another. You will have many disappointments and losses in trade; many ill-willed competitors.

LACE.—If a young man dreams that his sweetheart is adorned with lace, it shows to him that she will be very extravagant and improvident, and unfit to manage a house. She will be a regular dolly.

LADDER.—Brennius Salustis says, "This dream has great import. Art thou young and dreamest that thou hast reached the top of the ladder, thou hast a bright prospect before thee, and thou shalt attain it. Thou shalt kiss in wedlock thy coveted bride, or thy longed-for bridegroom. Man of commerce, it speaks well for thee. The breezes of fortune will blow thee into the harbour of independance. It is the portent of wealth, honour and human glory. Thou tiller of the ground, dost thou dream of reaching the top of the ladder? Thy grounds will bring forth plentifully, and make thee rich. Scholar, student, collegian, up, up, you will reach the climax of your ambition. And thou poor widow, thou, if thou dreamest this, shalt light thy coal again, and thy sorrow shall be turned into joy, but if when thou gettest to the top, and lookest down, and it maketh thee dizzy, it shows that thou wilt not be able to bear preferment; it will make thee proud and arrogant, and thou wilt tumble back into thy former hole of obscurity, Or if the ladder should break as thou goest up, thy hopes will be shipwrecked."

LAKE.—To dream of sailing on a smooth glassy lake, denotes future comfortable circumstances—a happy, pleasing life. It denotes success in business, and all honourable employments. It portends a large but agreeable family. It shows that the lover will be successful, and safely glide into agreeable matrimony. But if the water of the lake appears thick and muddy, it is indicative of much trouble and suffering arising from losses, insolvencies, &c.

LAMBS.—It is always favourable to dream of lambs.

If it be a young woman that dreams, it foretells her that her future husband will be of a sprightly, active disposition, very happy; that she will have many children, who will be healthy, and rise up to honour. If a young man it shows that his future wife will be young, very beautiful and virtuous, but rather inexperienced, and artless, and will need much experience to make her a good housewife. To those who are married, it shows that they will be happy in their children, though they will not escape the attacks of disease.

LAME.—To dream that you are lame implies that your future life will be one of difficulties and disappointments, and that your means of subsistence will be very limited and precarious. Your life will indeed be a warfare.

LAMENT.—To dream that you are lamenting any loss in trade, or by death, is a dream of contrary, you will have cause to rejoice on account of the acquisition [of some property, or the good conduct of your children. To dream that you hear others lamenting denotes good luck to your friends or relatives and that you will rejoice with them. I apprehend too that it is the precursor of a wedding.

LAMPS.—If you dream that you are carrying a bright lamp, it foretells that in your particular calling you will succeed, and be highly esteemed. To the lover it is a good omen. If you dream that you carry a lamp with a dim flickering light, it denotes your sickness; if the light goes out as you carry it, it portends your death, or, at least, the failure of your plans and hopes. To the lover it implies the death of love in the beloved. To dream of seeing many bright lamps denotes a coming festivity. If you appear to be exultant on the occasion, it denotes your marriage.

LAND.—To dream that you possess land is a good dream. It is indicative of wealth and independence. To dream that you give notice to quit land, foretells change of residence, probably in a far country. If you dream that you receive a notice to quit, it betokens reduced circumstances.

LARK.—It is very lucky to dream that you hear the singing of a lark. It denotes good health and prosperity. If not married it shows that your future partner will be rich, and that you will live in the country, and will have many children who will be virtuous, and a credit to you while you live. In all probability, some of your children will be talented musicians and vocalists.

LAUGHING.—To dream that you are laughing immoderately denotes vexation and disappointment. If you are in love it is a certain sign that you will not be reciprocated. The affection of your lover is not decided; it oscillates between you and another. Therefore be cautious how you act. Curb the passion of love; you are likely to be jilted. Laughing is often a sign of weeping and sorrow.

LAUREL.—To dream of Laurel, betokens victory and pleasure. If you marry it foretells possessions by your wife. It foreshows great prosperity. If a woman dreams of it and smells it, it denotes that she will bear children; to a maid, it shows speedy marriage.

LAW.—If you dream that you have a lawsuit, a suit in chancery, or any other case of litigation, it prognosticates very heavy losses in business, and many great difficulties; after such a dream it will be very hazardous to enter into any partnership, compact, security, or bond with any person. Be careful not to lend money, not to make any purchase immediately after such a dream, or you will have cause to regret your incautiousness.

LEAD.—To dream of lead denotes many troubles and quarrels. If in love there will be contention between you and your lover. If married it denotes that the affections of your partner are on the decline. It also foretells family quarrels, and separation, and great discomfort. It foretells to the sailor, or to a person about to take a voyage, that they will have a stormy voyage, that they will suffer shipwreck, and have a narrow escape from drowning.

LEAVES.—Dreaming you see the trees covered with beautiful fresh leaves, is good. Your affairs will prosper. You will succeed in business. It is a rare good dream for the lover, indicating full and continued affection. If you dream you see blossoms, and then fruit among the leaves, it denotes your marriage, and a numerous progeny. If the leaves appeared withered, ready to fall off, it is not a good omen; it portends losses in trade, bad crops to the farmer, disappointments in love, loss of friends by unfaithfulness, or death.

LEARNING.—To dream of being in a place of learning shows that you will attain influence and respect by your future diligence. It is a good omen to dream that you are learning, and easily acquire knowledge.

LEAPING.—If you dream of leaping over any impediment, it denotes that you will easily surmount every obstacle to advancement, and eventually rise to honour and affluence. Persevere, and the victory is sure. To persons in love, it shows many impediments and dangers, and also rivals; but if you dream that you leap over any obstacle, it foretells that you will win those whom you love, and be happy.

LEASE.—To dream of taking a house, shop, warehouse, or any other building on lease, foretells great success in trade, and that you will soon live together in marriage with the object of your affections.

LEECH.—To dream you see leeches applied denotes sickness. To dream one bites you, foretells that you will be greatly injured by some one.

LEG.—To dream you have bruised, dislocated, or broken your leg, or lost the use of it, foretells that a young woman will marry a man of intemperate and indolent habits, and who, through his improvident and unsteady conduct, will be always in poverty. It shows to a young man that he will marry a tender-hearted female, but rather irritable, and not a good manager in house affairs.

LEGACY.—The old astrologers declare this to be a lucky dream, always prognosticating the reception of some good fortune. The lovers' union will be a happy one; secular pursuits will be successful; farming occupations, and sea-faring engagements will prosper.

LEMONS.—To dream you see lemons growing on a tree denotes that you will visit a foreign land, and probably marry a native of it. To dream that you eat lemons denotes you will be attacked by a dangerous disease, from which it will be well if you recover. To dream you see a great number of lemons, denotes that your marriage, though pleasant for a while, will greatly disappoint your expectations.

LENDING.—This is not a good dream. You will be surrounded by a good many needy dependants, and by them annoyed, if not, impoverished. It is the omen of losses and great poverty.

LEOPARD. — To dream of these beautiful, yet savage creatures, indicates travel to a foreign land, where you will have to encounter many dangers and difficulties. But you will eventually overcome them, marry well, and be very prosperous and happy. It is likely that you will stay there all your life.

LEPROSY.—To dream that you have the leprosy, is always the forerunner of great troubles and misfortunes. It may also imply that you have been guilty of some crime tending to sorrow and disgrace, and probably imprisonment. You will have many enemies, some of whom will be very near to you.

LETTER.—Dreaming of receiving a letter sometimes indicates presents, or at least the reception of unexpected news, from a person you have not heard of for many years. To dream that you send a letter, denotes that you will soon be able to perform a generous action.

LICE.—This dream foretells much sickness, poverty and tribulation. Yourself, or some one to whom you are tenderly attached will meet with severe affliction, also expect much trouble in your business; it will fall off considerably, or if you are a servant, or manual labourer, it is probable you will lose your situation. This dream frequently prognosticates imprisonment for debt.

LIGHT.—To dream you see a light, of a brilliant

nature, denotes riches and honour; if you see it suddenly extinguished, it denotes a reversion in your affairs.

LIGHTNING.—It is a favourable dream, for it augurs success in business and advancement to honour and independence. To the farmer it portends propitious seasons, and abundant, and well-harvested crops. It is a good dream for the sailor; it foretells fair winds and a quick voyage. To those in love it denotes constancy in affection, and a speedy and happy marriage. If the lightning be attended with storm, rain, hail, and thunder, the dream is a bad one.

LILY.—To dream you see this lovely flower, it is a sign that by your virtuous and industrious career, you will be very happy and prosperous. To the lover it denotes the virtue of the object beloved. The lily is the emblem of purity; therefore it augurs well. If you marry, you will be happy, and have lovely children. If in your dream, you see the lily wither, then your most ardent expectations will be nullified. It portends failure, the death of a lover, a partner, a child, &c.

LINEN.—To dream that you are dressed in clean white linen, denotes that you will shortly receive some good tidings; that your intended is faithful and sincere, and will soon bring matters to a point. It is an omen of great success in business, and of large crops to the farmer, and of domestic felicity. If your linen appears in your dream to be chequered, you are likely to have a legacy left you. If it appears to be dirty, it is the omen of poverty, sickness, wretchedness, and want; also disappointment in love, rivalry, jealousy, &c.

LION.—This dream denotes greatness, future elevation. You will occupy some important and honourable position. To a young woman it foretells that she will be married to a man of noble bearing, superior intellect, and amiable disposition. To a young man, it denotes that his future wife will be no waster, but intellectual, of great spirit, and efficient in household affairs. She will be a help-meet for him indeed.

LIQUORS.—To dream that you drink brandy, is a certain sign that you will emigrate to, and reside in a foreign land, in improved circumstances. If you dream that you drink rum, it portends that you are to be a "sailor's bride," or the bride of one who obtains his livelihood by shipping. If you dream that you drink gin, it foretells that you will live in a large and populous town, and there be the subject of poverty and debt; it foretells great trade losses, and also the loss of your character. Dreaming of drinking whisky prognosticates a sudden reversion in your circumstances, loss of valuable friendships, and the world's scorn of you. You will need more than human support.

LIVERY SERVANTS.—To dream of livery servants, portends that you will soon emerge from your present obscurity, and associate with the wealthy and influential, for which you will be qualified by your possession of wealth. In matters of love it foretells that you will marry a person of independent circumstances, in whose affectionate esteem, you will be very happy indeed.

LOCK.—To dream of locks implies that difficulties will hinder your success. If you see cabinets, drawers, &c., with locks and no keys, it is a bad dream for the tradesman, and for the lover. You cannot effect your object. Your hope is sweet but it will never ripen into fruition. Should you dream that you find keys which open the locks, that circumstance completed, changes the omen of your dream. You will succeed—you will acquire—you will rise. Young woman, or young man, the heart of your lover is in captivity to you. It cannot swerve. Cherish it lovingly therefore.

LOOKING-GLASS.—To dream that you look at yourself in a mirror, indicates that your business is not conducted on sound principles, and must ultimately fail, if you do not properly arrange it. It indicates also that you are surrounded with deceitful persons, whom you will soon discover. In trying to injure you, they unmask themselves. Do not be too confiding, nor be led away by flattery. While you are not suspicious, by rather discriminating. Try to discover motives. And thou who lovest, beware of that rival; he is determined to supplant thee, and it is very likely he will succeed; he will soon show the cloven-foot, though now thou art fascinated by his sugared words to thee.

LOCOMOTIVE.—To dream of a railway-engine, foretells travel, or the arrival of some dear friend.

LOAD.—To dream that you are carrying a heavy load, under which you groan and tremble, foretells that your future life will be one of care and toil. Great difficulties will encompass your paths, many obstructions to your happiness. But if in your dream you are able to carry your load, and carry it to the appointed place safely, then it augurs, you will rise above all your difficulties and troubles, and pass the rest of your days in ease and comfort.

LOTTERY.—To dream of being in a lottery is a

dream of warning to young persons, cautioning them not to be precipitate in giving their hearts to an apparent lover, they are sure to meet with disappointment and vexations. After such a dream, a female ought to consult her friends on the prospects of marriage, and be guided by their advice. A young man ought to be very careful on whom he sets his affections, for this dream foretells that he will be tempted to form an attachment to a female who will render him very unhappy, for she will be overbearing, unamiable, a great scold, fond of drink, and addicted to gossip, and spreading scandalous reports. How true is the addage, "Marriage is a lottery with more blanks than prizes."

LOVE.—To dream that you see *Cupid*, the god of love, and that he smites you with his arrow, is a sign that some one loves you, who will soon declare himself; and the same dream denotes the same to a young man. To dream you do not succeed in love is a dream of contrary; you will succeed, and marry, and be happy. To dream that your friends love you, foretells future prosperity in business, and great domestic happiness. To dream of being in company with your lover is a good dream. You will soon marry the object of your choice, have many children, who will be to you a source of comfort and joy. To a woman with child it foretells a safe delivery of a lovely child. To dream of loving and being loved, denotes that you will enjoy a large circle of loving friends ready to assist you in any emergency, and be faithful at all times. It foretells to the farmer propitious seasons, heavy crops and much wealth. The sailor will have several good voyages, in the last of which he will marry a rich female, and become settled in life.

LUCKY.—To dream that you are lucky is a dream of contrary. It is the omen of disappointment, and misfortune. After such a dream, be cautious, and keep your eyes open. Let judgment, and not your passions, rule.

LUGGAGE.—If you dream that you are travelling, and that you are encumbered and annoyed with a great deal of heavy luggage, it foretells great trials and difficulties which will cause you much trouble and expense. This will almost overwhelm you, and you will be in great straits, principally caused by embarrassment, or insolvency of others, or the injustice and bad treatment of some of your relatives. To a lover it denotes the delicate health of a future wife or husband, which will be a source of great expense. To a traveller, it foretells danger and disaster.

LUMBER.—To dream that you are surrounded and annoyed with lumber, foretells misfortune and trouble. To dream that you are searching among lumber, and find something valuable, foretells the acquisition of a fortune, which will completely reverse your circumstances.

LUTE.—To dream that you hear the sweet tones of a lute, foretells the receipt of good news from a long absent friend, or from one whom you ardently love. It also denotes to the lover that the person beloved is true, of amiable and engaging manners, and great sweetness of disposition. To a young woman it shows that her lover is devotedly attached to her, and is good tempered, sincere, and constant, but not very rich. They will marry, and have lovely children who will do well, and be their solace in the time of old age. Such a dream foretells a happy old age and good health; and in all cases it is the fore-runner of success and happiness.

LUXURY.—To dream of living in great luxury is a sign of sickness and poverty, and that you will meet with many disappointments. You are not likely to be successful in trade; you will have many crosses, great losses, and be in danger of imprisonment for debt. In love it denotes rivalry, jealousy, and quarrels, between lovers, and to them that are married it foretells disobedient and refractory children, and much family strife and contention.

MACHINERY.—To dream that you are inspecting machinery, and it affords you pleasure, foretells that your trade will prosper, and that you will have to extend your operations to supply the demands of your customers. And thus you will rapidly grow rich, and be honoured by those around you. To a female who dreams that she sees her future husband among machinery, shows that her lover is of industrious habits, and although not now rich, he will ultimately become so.

MACKEREL.—To dream that you see these fishes in the water very clearly, foretells success in trade, prosperity and good fortune. If you dream of stinking mackerel you will never marry your present sweetheart, for she will prove worthless, being false-hearted.

MADNESS.—To dream you are mad, or in company with mad persons, portends well for the dreamer; even vigour of intellect, great efficiency in commercial transactions and adequate remuneration, even to the acquisition of wealth. The merchant, the tradesman, the sea-captain, the farmer, after such a dream may expect an uncommon tide of prosperity. It also betokens good health and long life. "Young persons have asked me about this dream," says old Ptolemy, "and I have invariably told them it was a good ominous dream. Young man, you will find a maiden just to your mind, and right happy in wedlock shalt thou be. Young woman, thy future husband shall be all that thou canst wish; intelligent, wise, industrious, persevering, loving, and ready to die for thee. And all my interpretations have been correct."

MAGIC.—Dreaming of magic foretells changes and revolutions. Some change will take place in your circumstances, but it will be a change for the better. Like magic your present poverty and wretchedness will disappear, and your throbbing heart will be at rest soon. But it indicates also that your hitherto trusted friend will be unmasked by acts of treachery and injustice, but you will triumph over that enemy. Your present love, and that of your sweetheart, will abide only a little longer. Both of you wish for a change. Quick, pass, begone! it is better to be so; and so you will think by and by.

MAGISTRATE.—To dream that you stand charged with crime before a magistrate, it is bad, if he convict you; if he pronounces you free, the dream is ominous of good. If you dream that you are raised to the magistracy, it foretells future advancement to a high official station, with great honour, and large emoluments.

MAGNET.—To dream that you see a number of magnets foretells that your path will be laid with snares; mind you are not ensnared with such fascinations. If you dream that you are using a magnet, it indicates that you are plotting and planning against some one to bring them under your power for selfish purposes. If you see others using the magnet, and you see your lover near, depend upon it you have rivals, who will leave no stone unturned to get you into their power. Beware of such. If a maiden sees her lover using a magnet it portends the hollowness of his heart, his language to be insincere, and all his vows, and sighs, and declarations, to be utterly worthless. His intentions are quite dishonourable, therefore shun such company.

MAGPIE.—To dream that you see a magpie, foretells that you will soon be married, but that you will lose your partner in a few years after your union, To dream you see two magpies, it denotes that you will be married twice, and be twice widowed. And if a man dreams that he sees three magpies, it portends the death of his wife in childbed, and also the death of the child.

MALT.—To dream that you are brewing malt into beer is a sign of marriage, and much domestic enjoyment. To dream that you see a large quantity of malt in a maltkiln, and purchase it, is the omen of great prosperity, and of long life, and a comfortable old age. If a female dreams of malt it is likely that she will marry a publican who will become a great drunkard. If a woman with child dreams of malt, the child will be a male, and he will grow up to be a drunkard.

MANNA.—To dream of manna is rather a fortunate dream, denoting that though the journey of life will be chequered, yet there will be many comforts to sweeten its bitters; there will be light in darkness, and the conquest of every difficulty.

MANSLAUGHTER.—To dream that you have been

guilty of manslaughter, foretells misunderstandings, family jars and quarrels. You will disagree with a very intimate friend. It also denotes rivalry in love, and very angry, if not violent contentions, and the separation of lovers. It foretells losses in business, and probably insolvency. It is a bad dream predicting robbery, fire, destruction of property and life on land and on sea.

MANUFACTORY.—To dream that you are inspecting a factory, when all is in operation, denotes that your trade will flourish, by which you will acquire much wealth, and be very useful all your life. It also betokens a time of commercial prosperity generally.

MAP.—To dream that you are inspecting a map indicates that you will have to leave your native land and reside many years in a foreign country, but eventually you will return to your own country. If you inspect a plain map you will return poor; but if it be a coloured map, you will come back very wealthy, which will make you happy in old age. If a female inspects a map in her dream, it indicates that her husband and her sons will be great travellers.

MARIGOLDS.—To dream of marigolds denotes a constant lover, and a happy marriage; also elevation in circumstances, accumulation of riches and honours, and great success in your undertakings and constancy in love.

MARINER.—To dream that you are a mariner, intimates that very likely you will have to emigrate to some distant part. To dream you see a number of mariners, portends news from abroad; and to the man of business it indicates successful bargains and seafaring transactions. If a young woman dreams of mariners, and one in particular, it foretells that a sailor will be her husband; if she dreams of a mariner in distress at sea by storms, &c., it is a dream of contrary; her husband will safely return.

MARKET.—To dream that you are in a market, marketing, denotes a good trade, competent circumstances, and high domestic enjoyment. It denotes some approaching happy event, which will be the cause of joy and feasting. If a female dreams that she is in a market, where many look at her, it is a sign she will have many lovers, and it will be difficult for her to decide which to take.

MARMALADE.—To dream that you are eating marmalade alone, portends personal sickness. If you dream that you are eating it with other persons, it indicates that you will meet with many kind friends who will ever be ready to comfort and cheer you. To dream that you eat marmalade with only one person, portends that the soft speech, and sugared words of your lover are likely to deceive you. Beware of mere pretenders. To dream that you make marmalade, denotes a wedding at which you will be prominent.

MARRIAGE.—To dream you see a marriage is a sign of an interment in which you are interested. To dream you are married is ominous of death. It is very unfavourable to the dreamer; it denotes poverty, a prison, misfortune, and the alienation of a lover. To dream that you assist at a wedding, portends some pleasing news, indicating advancement in life for you. To the sailor the dream of marriage augurs storms, and shipwrecks, and narrow escape from death.

MARSH.—To dream that you are walking in a marshy country, portends a troubled life. If you can scarcely get along for swamps, it denotes many sorrows and difficulties. But if you get on easily and out of the marsh soon, it foretells that the remnant of your days will be passed in moderate comfort. To the lover this dream shows many scrapes and trials, but ultimate triumph over every impediment and foe.

MARTYR.—To dream of the age of the martyrs denotes that you will be firmly attached to the verities of the Christian religion, and be in intimate alliance with the excellent of the earth. To dream that you are a martyr, is indicative of your unwavering defence of the truth, and your triumph over all hostility.

MASK.—Should a young person dream that his or her lover appears to them wearing a mask, it is a sure sign of insincerity and deceit. It shows double dealing, a pretending of love to you, while engaged to marry another. Learn to discriminate and to ascertain motives.

MASTIFF.—To dream you see a mastiff, is a sure sign that some one whom you suspect of infidelity is, after all, your best friend. If you dream that you are bitten by a mastiff, it prognosticates that some pretended friends will greatly injure you, especially in love affairs; they will anxiously strive to supplant you in the affections of your sweetheart. If a maid dreams of a mastiff, it shows that her lover is faithful and true.

MAY-POLE.—To dream that you dance round the May-pole, or that you are watching others dance round one, announces the advent of some joyous occasion. It also foretells a long and happy life, that you will never want, but always have a competence ; neither poverty nor riches. It also foretells that a maiden will marry a sober and industrious person, with whom she will be very happy, and by whom she will have a numerous family. Their children will rise up healthy and strong, virtuous and happy, and will not forsake them in time of old age. If a widow dreams of dancing round a May-pole it foretells that she will marry again.

MEADOW.—To dream that you are walking through a meadow, predicts good fortune to you. If a maiden dreams that she is walking with a young man in a meadow, it is a sign that her beau will be very loving, that he will marry her, and acquire riches, and by him she will have a numerous and beautiful family, and will be very happy and live long. To a young man, it denotes that he will marry a beautiful and rich young lady, who will be devotedly attached to him, and be his constant solace. They will have a numerous family characterised by honour and happiness.

MEASLES.—To dream that you are ill of the measles, denotes that riches are about to drop into your lap from a quarter which you did not expect to yield any thing. It also implies returning health, and business prosperity.

MEDICINE.—To dream that you are taking medicine, and it tastes nauseous to the palate, implies that something will occur to you that will be very annoying and unpleasant for a little time only, and then be of much service to you. The dark clouds will vanish, and light appear. Rest will follow toil, and pleasure pain. It is a good dream.

MELONS.—A young man, or a young woman who dreams of melons is destined to marry or be married to a rich foreigner, and to live in a foreign land. Such a union will be crowned with great happiness, be attended with great wealth ; their children will be few, but they will be virtuous and happy.

MENDICANT.—To dream that you are a beggar is a dream of contrary. You will amass wealth, and be far above the reach of poverty. You will marry a person comparatively poor ; but she will be a virtuous woman, whose price is above rubies. To dream that you are accosted in the street by a beggar, denotes great trouble through a seeming friend, who however can do you no harm.

METALS.—To dream of gold denotes great trials, sickness, loss of property, and pecuniary embarrassment. To dream of silver foretells that you will meet with deceitful persons, and disappointment in love. To dream of copper coins, denotes poverty, and to dream of the metal, denotes shipwrecks and accidents during travelling. To dream of iron indicates that you will marry a person of great spirit, and that you will acquire great wealth through your own industry, and successful speculations. To dream of lead portends the loss of your lover or the death of some beloved friend or relation.

MICE.—To dream of mice indicates many intermeddling enemies and slanderers, also poverty and unsuccessful undertakings. It also foretells an unfortunate marriage and disobedient children.

MICROSCOPE.—To dream that you are looking through a microscope, denotes that you will discover some lurking and deceitful enemy, who will appear to you in real character, no longer under a disguise ;

also that you will be separated from your lover by removal to a distance; but you will meet again in happy wedlock, and have a numerous progeny.

MILK.—To dream that you drink milk, foretells joy. To dream of selling milk, denotes bad trade, and disappointments in love. To dream that you give milk, denotes prosperity, and a happy marriage. To dream that you see it flowing from a woman's breast, denotes marriage, and a very large family. To dream of milking a cow, foretells great plenty to the farmer, healthy cattle, and abundant crops.

MIMIC.—To dream you hear a ludicrous imitation, indicates that you will meet with a mere pretender to pecuniary ability; one on whom it would not be safe to depend, or to trust. It portends also that you will have a lover whose intentions respecting you are quite dishonourable. Endeavour, therefore, to find out motives.

MINCE-PIES.—To dream of eating mince-pies intimates that you will have to be at a wedding. To dream that you are making mince-pies, portends that you will soon be making preparations for your marriage. Your partner will be tolerably well off, though not affluent.

MISER.—This is an unfavourable dream. It foretells bad success through life, and great troubles. You will never rise above your present circumstances, but probably become poorer and more wretched. In love it foretells marriage with a person who will make you miserable by low despicable ways, and that you will have many bad children.

MISFORTUNE.—To dream that some misfortune has happened to you or your lover, is a dream of contrary, foretelling that a person will be very fortunate in business, and have a very happy selection of a lover. You will rise in life, and be greatly respected and esteemed. In married life you will be very comfortable; your children will be numerous, healthy, and a source of comfort to you.

MONEY.—To dream that you pay money, foretells your competency to do it through a prosperous business. To dream that you receive money foretells the birth of a child, or the gain of a law-suit; it generally portends prosperity. To dream you find money foretells sudden advancement through a prosperous business and by marriage.

MOON.—To dream of the moon, foretells unexpected joy, and success in love. If it be a new moon it is a good dream for the tradesman, and farmer, and lover. The full moon denotes marriage; it is good for a widow.

MOTHS.—To dream of moths indicates enemies, who are doing you great injury, and labouring to undermine your position in life. It also portends that your lover will hear reports about you that will cause a quarrel between you, and probably a separation. To persons in trade it indicates that you have dishonest and unfaithful servants who are injuring you in your business.

MOTHER.—To dream that you see your mother and converse pleasantly with her, denotes your comfort and prosperity through life. If a female, who has a lover, dreams that she has become a mother, it is a sad dream. To dream that you lose your mother, denotes her sickness.

MOUNTAIN.—To dream that you are ascending a steep and rugged mountain, shows a life of toil and sorrow; all your endeavours to better yourself will be thwarted by unforeseen events, as afflictions, losses, &c., and it is to be feared that you will never rise in the world, for calamities will come thick upon you.

MOURNING.—This is a dream of contrary. It portends good concerning you. Your lover is genuine, entirely devoted to you, and is sure to marry you, and to make you very happy. To the married it denotes much comfort, and to the merchant, tradesman, and sea-faring man, it denotes great prosperity. The farmer will reap abundantly.

MURDER.—To dream that you have committed murder, is an awfully portentous dream. It foretells your vicious life, the perpetration of evil, and probably imprisonment. After such a dream, repent and abandon sin and evil associations, or it will be dreadful for you. To the tradesman and farmer, it foretells many grievous losses, by failures and robbery. It denotes that your lover will prove false.

MUSHROOMS. — To dream that you are eating mushrooms denotes personal sickness. To dream that you are gathering them, foretells the accumulation of wealth.

MUSIC.—To dream you hear delicious music is a very favourable omen; it denotes joyful news from a long absent friend; to married people it denotes sweet-tempered children; in love, it shows that your sweetheart is very fond of you. Rough and discordant music denotes trouble and vexation.

MYRTLE.—To dream you see a beautiful and fragrant myrtle, denotes agreeable circumstances. To a young person it foretells a very suitable and agreeable lover, a very pleasant courtship, leading to the altar of Hymen. It portends a legacy to the dreamer. If a married person dreams of a myrtle-tree, it foretells that he or she will be married twice, and the second time to a person who has been married before. Also, you will have a very numerous family, the most of which will live to maturity and grow wealthy.

NAKED.—To dream that you are naked is a bad omen, foretelling poverty, disgrace, and misfortune. If you are engaged in business, it is a sign that you will fail, become bankrupt, and very narrowly escape imprisonment. If you are in the sea-faring line, expect storms, shipwreck, and great sufferings. If you are a farmer, you will have bad crops, and you will lose many of your cattle, and suffer by robbery. To lovers it foretells that they will never marry those whom they now address; but another person of disagreeable temper, arbitrary, selfish, and tyrannical. The imprudence and self-gratification of such a person will inevitably produce ruin. To married persons it foretells infidelity in a partner, great misery, and very disobedient children.

NAME.—To dream that you have changed your name, is a sign that you will never be married.

NECKLACE.—To dream that you are wearing a rich and costly necklace, most surely portends that you will speedily make a conquest of a very wealthy person; the courtship will pleasantly continue, till consummated by happy wedlock. Numerous beautiful children, mostly females, will be the pledges of pure and sincere affection. They will all grow up very beautiful and marry rich men. If a female dreams that she breaks the necklace and loses the beads, her children will die young, and she will become poor in her old age.

NECTAR.—To dream that you are drinking nectar foretells that you will accumulate riches and honour, and that you will rise beyond your most sanguine expectations. It also shows that you will marry a handsome person in high life and live in great state, to an old age.

NEST (*of Birds.*)—Dreaming of a bird's nest, prognosticates marriage and domestic happiness. You will have a comfortable nest with many young ones in it, who will be honourable and creditable to you. To a sailor it foretells that he will find a rich wife and a happy home at the next port he enters; and to the tradesman it presages great success, and consequent independence; to the farmer it predicts a plentiful harvest. If you dream of a bird's nest having broken eggs, or dead birds, it is a bad dream, betokening failure and distress.

NETTLES.—To dream of nettles prognosticates good health, and worldly prosperity; but to dream that you are stung by nettles indicates vexation and disappointment. You will be deeply hurt by the ungrateful conduct of some pretended friend; and if you are in love, your sweetheart will be tempted to deceive you and to marry your rival.

NEWSPAPER.—Dreaming that you are reading a newspaper shows that you will hear from a distant friend good news, which will cause you to quit your present employment, but you will succeed much better for the change. You will be exalted above common servitude, and be able to commence business

on your own account, in which you will have great
success, and amass great riches. If you are a single
man, it portends that you will marry a widow, and
that you will have an expensive lawsuit which never-
theless will end in your favour. To persons in love
it shows that the object of their affections will remove to a distant part of the world, and it will be
many years before they are again united, but their
reunion will be a very happy one. To the politician,
it betokens great and stirring events in the nation.
To the farmer it shows a favourable season and an
advance in the price of grain.   To the sailor a prosperous and quick voyage.

NIGHT.—To dream that night suddenly overtakes
you, denotes a great change in your situation ; a
change from competency to want and dark adversity.
To dream that you are walking on a dark night,
denotes grief and disappointment, losses and misfortunes.   If you are in business, you will have many
losses and bad debts, and probably become insolvent,
and be sent to prison. If you are a farmer, you will
suffer bad crops and a loss of some of your best
cattle ; and if you are a sailor, it denotes a stormy
voyage and a miserably small freight. To those who
are in love it foretells some very unpleasant misunderstandings and contentions with your sweetheart
which will most likely end in a separation.   If you
are married, it indicates that your partner is unfaithful to you, and friendly with an intimate friend and
companion.

NIGHTINGALE.—To dream of hearing this sweet-
singing bird, is a very propitious omen, and may
always be regarded as the harbinger of joy, success,
and prosperity.   It is a good dream for persons in

adversity, or for the sick; as it betokens a reverse of their state. It is a sign that a single person will meet with a lover, whose person, manners, intellectual qualities and acquirements, will be very enchanting. The exclamation will be, " How sweet is thy voice, and thy countenance is comely." Young person, you could not have a better dream. You will be admired and be greatly loved. You will be married, and have children; some of them will possess great vocal powers, and all of them will be a comfort to you. To dream that you hear the nightingale indicates that all your undertakings will be successful. Good fortune will await you; probably advancement to some high and lucrative position.

NIGHTMARE.—To dream that you have the night-mare signifies that you are under the influence of a foolish and imprudent person.

NINEPINS.—To dream of playing at this game implies great fluctuation and reverses in business, caused by heavy losses. You will be reduced in your state, and have to struggle with great poverty. It also denotes hollow-hearted friendships, false lovers, and disappointments in love and marriage.

NOISES.—To dream of hearing great and alarming noises foretells domestic quarrels and dissensions; and much misery in consequence. You will be alienated from your best friends and lose the esteem of your relatives. If you are a lover, it portends that through bad influence, your intended will abandon you.

NOSE BLEEDING.—To dream that you are bleeding at the nose, denotes that you will have sickness, and your life be in danger. To persons in trade it denotes bad trade and heavy losses. If you are engaged in a trial or lawsuit it portends that you will be cast with expenses, which will almost overwhelm you. If you are in love you may expect that your lover will prove unfaithful to you and marry your most intimate friend. It also forebodes contentions and separations in your own family, which will greatly distress you for a season; but afterwards the breach will be healed, and happiness return. Such a dream should warn you not to travel for some time after this dream, as it prognosticates accidents, nor to enter into any new undertaking; above all to avoid lending money, or you will lose both the money and the friendship of those to whom you lend it.

NOSEGAY.—To dream that a person gives you a nosegay, shows friendship. If you dream a young man gives you one, it is a sign that you will have a very agreeable lover; If you dream that you give one to a young woman, it denotes that your addresses will be agreeable, and you will be accepted.

NUISANCE.—To dream you see a nuisance and that you have to remove it, denotes that your life will be disagreeable, and one of drudgery. If you dream that another person has committed a nuisance, you will soon hear of the disgrace and degradation of an acquaintance.

NUN.—For a young female to dream that she has entered a nunnery, and become a nun, prognosticates disappointment in love, and that she will experience much sorrow, almost driving her mad. It also warns her to beware of seduction, and not to put undue confidence in the faith of man. Strive to investigate the motives which actuate him.

NUTS.—To dream of nuts having good kernels, is

a good omen, denoting that you will become wealthy through the possession of a good legacy, and that you will marry an agreeable and rather affluent person, and rear a numerous and happy family, that you will live to a good old age, and be highly respected by a large circle of friends and acquaintances.

OAK.—To dream of a large oak with beautiful foliage is a very good dream. To the man of business it indicates a steady and permanent trade, and that you will be able to endure and surmount all trials. To a family it denotes constant and abiding domestic happiness. It also forebodes a happy, hale, and robust old age. To a young man it portends that he will commence business and succeed, and that he will marry a pretty and intelligent woman, of courageous and resolute disposition, very efficient in domestic management, very industrious, and having a very amiable disposition. To a young woman, it foreshows that her future husband will be handsome, having a strong and robust constitution ; he will be very temperate, industrious, and decided for the support and enjoyment of his family, and especially for their education and moral training. To dream of an oak full of acorns, foretells of unbounded prosperity. To dream of a withered and decayed oak indicates that your brightest prospects will be blasted, while the latter part of your life will be full of poverty and loss. A blasted oak foretells sudden death.

OATS.—For a farmer to dream that he sees fine oats in the fields, or otherwise, it portends a bountiful harvest, and a sunny time for reaping the same. For a merchant, it augurs successful commercial enterprise ; and it indicates to the tradesman a flourishing business ; to all, that their plans shall succeed. To the young man about to commence business, it is a good omen; he will succeed in gaining a fortune by industry and perseverance. If intending to travel, it is a favourable omen; the traveller, and the sailor will have a safe and lucrative journey. If you are engaged in a lawsuit with any one, it indicates that the result will be in your favour. If you are single, and dream that you are walking with a person through a field of green oats, it is a sign that your intended is only simple and inexperienced; it through a field of ripe oats, it denotes your intended to have a good intellect, and ardent and sincere intentions. You will soon be married, and have an interesting family.

OCEAN.—To dream that you gaze upon the ocean when it is calm, is good; when it is stormy and turbid, it augurs ill. To dream of sailing on the ocean when it is smooth, and the weather calm, with favourable breezes, certainly denotes the accomplishment of a purpose, designs answered, and the object devoutly wished for, obtained. After such a dream happiness and satisfaction will follow. It prognosticates success in love affairs. To lovers, it foreshows that they will have a delicious courtship, and sail straight and honourably on into the harbour of matrimony. Your wishes will meet in one another, and you will have mutual and endearing affection. To the sailor, this is a dream of contrary, if he dreams of a pleasant voyage, it denotes a stormy and unsuccessful voyage; if he dreams of a stormy voyage, it portends the reverse, a fine, safe, and prosperous voyage.

OFFENCE.—To dream that some one has given you offence, certainly portends that some disagreeable altercations will take place between you and your lover, or between you and your most particular friend, which will end in cessation of intercourse and friendship, and which will not soon be made up. Beware of giving cause to others for offence, and be very guarded in your speech. If you have opinions of your own, do not try dogmatically to enforce them upon others. In your discussions be mild and persuasive, so that none may have an advantage over you. To dream that you are so offended as to seek revenge, or that an offended person is so disposed, beware, for there is danger that your passions may hurry yon away into difficulties, or that you may receive injury from another.

OFFICE.—To dream you are turned out of your office, foreshows death and loss of property; to a lover it indicates want of affection in your sweetheart, and misery if you marry the present object of your affections; to a sailor, it announces bad weather and shipwreck.

OLD MAN.—For a woman to dream she is courted by an old man, is a sure prognostic that she will receive a sum of money, and be successful in her undertaking. For a maid to dream of it, shows that she will marry a rich young fellow, will have many children by him, who will all become rich.

OLD WOMAN.—For a man to dream he is courting an old woman, and that she returns his love, is a very fortunate omen, it prefigures success in worldly concerns; that he will marry a beautiful young woman, have lovely children, and be very happy.

OLIVES.—To dream that you are gathering olives, denotes peace, delight, and happiness in domestic life, and in every situation. To dream that you are eating olives, it foretells that you will rise above your present circumstances, whatever they may be; that you will obtain the favour and patronage of influential men, who will cause you to fill a profitable government situation and acquire wealth. For a person in love to dream of olives, either gathering or eating them, foretells that the person who addresses you is characterized by cincerity and truth. You will have a happy conjugal life, attended with great prosperity.

ONIONS.—To dream that you are eating onions portends the discovery of a valuable treasure, or lost goods and money. To dream of paring onions and to have your eyes affected thereby, denotes quarrels with your friends, or with your family, which will be deeply affecting to you. To dream that you are getting onions, denotes that a friend will recover from sickness.

ORANGES.—This dream is generally unfavourable. It foretells personal and relative sickness and misfortune; also misunderstandings and family jars. To the lover, dreaming of oranges foretells coldness on the part of your lover, and growing indifference, and ultimate cruel abandonment of you. If you afterwards enter the marriage life, and dream about oranges, it denotes an unhappy marriage. In commerce, it foretells heavy losses through insolvency, and through the dishonesty of those employed. And to the farmer they indicate failure of crops, and other losses.

ORCHARD.—To dream that you are in an orchard, gathering fruit, agreeable to the taste, as well as pleasant to the eye, foretells that you will be made the heir to some property, and become rich. If the fruit appears ripe, your advancement will be immediate; if green, it is yet in the distance; but it will come.

ORGAN.—To dream that you see an organ, and hear it pealing beautiful anthems, &c., in a place of worship, predicts to persons in business great prosperity; to the sailor, a pleasant and prosperous voyage, and to the farmer a bountiful harvest. To persons in love it portends fortunate marriage, with very suitable persons, and children who will rise up to be blessings and ornaments in society.

OVEN.—To dream that you are baking in an oven, foretells moderate success in trade. But if you burn the bread, and it appears black, it portends disaster. Your trade will fail, and for a season, you will fall into poverty. It also denotes jealousy, rivalry, and quarrels among lovers, caused by an envious and undermining female, who is likely to succeed in causing separation.

OVERBOARD.—To dream that you have fallen overboard at sea, denotes sickness, poverty, imprisonment, and bad success in your undertakings. It also forewarns you that some friend, or perhaps your lover, will turn perfidious, act a strange deceitful part, and by duplicity and misrepresentations, cause you great grief and sorrow. You will be in danger of sinking under the trial; but you will eventually surmount it, and be happy in a true lover. To a farmer it prognosticates disease amongst his cattle, and his poultry. To the sailor it is a dream of contrary, foretelling a safe voyage to a distant part, and a safe arrival at home.

OWL.—To dream that you see this bird of night, and that you hear it howl, denotes sickness, poverty, and disgrace. After dreaming of an owl, never expect to meet with continued prosperity, or to marry your present lover, or to succeed in your present undertakings.

OX.—To dream that you see a herd of oxen is the harbinger of great prosperity and success in your engagements, particularly if you see them grazing, in which case it denotes the accumulation of immense wealth, and your elevation to honour and dignity. To lovers, it presages a happy and fortunate marriage, and that your partner will have a legacy left by a wealthy relative. To dream that you are pursued by an ox foretells that you will have an enemy or rival, who will much annoy you.

OYSTERS.—To dream of eating oysters foretells that after many conflicts, and heavy losses, you will acquire wealth and independance; that married persons shall enjoy domestic happiness, and that lovers by patiently waiting, shall obtain their wish by a happy conjugal alliance.

PAIN.—This is a dream of contrary. If you dream that you suffer great pain denotes the advent of some particular event, by which you will be greatly benefited. To persons in trade it foretells that there will be a great advance in the prices of some of the goods which they sell, by which advance they will realize considerable profits. To lovers it is an omen for good, foretelling the arrival of the propitious time when they will realize with partners possessing an ample fortune. To the farmer it foretells a very congenial and rich season, and that he will obtain a greater price for his product than ever he did; and to the sailor it prognosticates that he will marry a rich widow at the next port he touches at.

PALACE.—To dream that you live in a palace is a good omen, foreshowing that you will emerge from your present obscurity, and be elevated to a state of wealth and dignity. To the lover it portends an agreeable partner, and a very happy marriage.

PALM-TREE.—To dream that you see a palm-tree in full blossom, and smell its fragrance, is a very significant dream, in which case it predicts much success, prosperity and happiness to the dreamer, particularly in matters of love. Notwithstanding your fears and misgivings you will secure the affections of your lover never more to be alienated from you ; your love so mutual, shall be crowned with union at the altar. Children, the sweet pledges of your affection will gather around your table like olive-plants, and they will grow up to be useful and honoured while they live. It also foretells successful speculations, a flourishing trade ; deliverance from pecuniary difficulties, and the fortunate result of a lawsuit, a ripe old age, and much comfort to it.

PANCAKES.—To dream that you are eating pancakes denotes the fruition of hope, the arrival of some joyous occasion, that you have long been expecting. In matters of love it foretells that you will be shortly married, and that your partner will be loving, industrious, and frugal, and study to make you very happy. If you are trying to turn a pancake, and cannot succeed, it bespeaks loss in business, and failure in love.

PANTOMIME.—To dream that you witness a pantomime at a theatre, implies that you live among deceitful persons ; and that those who profess to be your friends, and flatter you, and speak well to your face, are deceitful in heart, and are labouring insiduously to injure you as much as they can. You will soon find them out, as in reference to business and love matters, they will shortly develop their real characters.

PAPER OR PARCHMENT.—To dream of paper or parchment implies that you will get into trouble, and most likely you will be accused of some crime that will cost a deal of money and anxiety before you can exculpate yourself. To dream that you can see clean paper, denotes that the affection of your friend or lover is unquestionably sincere. To dream of dirty, scribbled, or blotted paper shows the reverse; also unjust and dirty actions. If the paper is properly written on, it portends good bargains. If folded up, or crushed, it denotes disappointments; if neatly folded, that you will obtain your wish.

PARADISE.—This is certainly a good dream, denoting to married persons, a religious and happy life, patient endurance of all its sorrows, a bright hope of immortality, and, after the cessation of life, a sure and certain entrance into Paradise. To a young man, it foretells that his wife will be a virtuous woman, will have some property, will have many interesting children, and will be a help-meet for him in every sense. To a young woman, it foreshows that her husband will be an intellectual man, pious, and very indefatigable in business, and to produce domestic comfort. She will have very beautiful, healthy, and interesting children. They will be very good and obedient, and rise to eminency. This is a good dream for the farmer; portending abundant crops, and a glorious harvest. It is a good dream for the emigrant, denoting that the country in which he has decided to live will meet all his expectations, and that he will be very happy and prosperous there. To every one who dreams about Paradise, it is the omen of good.

PARCEL.—To dream that you receive a parcel denotes good fortune. You will either hear from a friend, or receive a present; if you dream that you are carrying a parcel through the streets, it denotes great changes in business, and a loss of custom, and greatly reduced circumstances. It also denotes disappointment in love matters, and that your lover will marry another person. If a lover dreams of receiving a parcel, it is a favourable omen, denoting success in love.

PARK.—To dream of walking through a park, indicates health and happiness, and true friendship. To a person in trade it is the harbinger of a flourishing business. If you dream that you have the company of another person with you, it denotes a true and faithful lover, and a speedy marriage. The now apparent obstacles will all vanish. Such a dream is very good for a scholar, or a person seeking perferment. It is also a propitious dream for the merchant, sailor, and farmer.

PARLIAMENT.—To dream that you are a member of the house of parliament, foretells advancement. To dream that you are only a visitor, and that you listen to the debates, foretells family quarrels and dissensions; also that you will quarrel with your sweetheart and friends.

PARROTS.—To dream you hear a parrot talk, foretells that you will have a very talkative person for your companion. To dream that you see many parrots foretells that you will emigrate to a foreign country, where you will settle and marry, and be very happy. You will cultivate land and by it amass great wealth, and secure great dignity and honour. You will only have two children, a boy and a girl; the latter will be married to a rich man ; and the former will become an official character, and be very useful and highly esteemed.

PARTRIDGE.—To dream that you see a flock or covey of partridges, foretells many troubles and misfortunes ; but if they fly away, it portends that you will overcome them all and be happy. Partridges also denote enemies and false friends who will endeavour to create prejudices against you, and to sow dissensions between you and your lover.

PASSING-BELL.—To dream that you hear the solemn knell of the passing bell, portends personal or relative sickness ; also misfortunes and great trouble. It also denotes your bereavement of a parent, or relative, or friend. It is not a favourable dream for a lover, as it denotes that he or she will not marry their present lover, but will have to mourn on account of his or her death. It portends no good fortune to the tradesman, nor to the farmer, nor to the sailor. Your present schemes will not be successful. In law, if you do abandon the lawsuit, you are sure to fail.

PATH.—Walking in a good path denotes success in trade, in farming, and in love matters ; if married, it denotes that a female will have a safe delivery, and that the whole family will be happy. If, in your dream, the path appears crooked, and filled occasionally with thorns, it foretells disappointments and treacherous friends.

PAWNBROKER.—To dream of being at a pawnbroker's pawning any article, foretells losses, misfortunes, troubles, and disappointments. It portends that you will have some quarrel or dispute with some person that will end in a trial or lawsuit, which will go against you, and nearly plunge you into ruin. If you are a lover it foretells that your sweetheart is unfaithful to you and prefers another, and that they will be married, to your great chagrin ; but despond not; the loss will be your gain, as you will sometime 'after be allied to a superior person. If you are after any office, situation, or appointment, this dream foretells that you will be an unsuccessful candidate.

PEACHES.—To dream that you are eating peaches, foretells personal sickness, which though very severe, will soon pass away, and you will be healthy and strong again. To dream that you see peaches growing, denotes deceit in love and friendship.

PEACOCK.—To dream that you see a Peacock with its feathers spread, denotes an unsound and uncertain position in life, and that you are surrounded with seeming friends, but who are deceitful. If you see the bird with its feathers not spread, it foretells a young man that he will marry a beautiful wife, and attain riches and honour ; and that a female will marry a handsome man, and live in ease and comfort, but she will have no children. To the farmer it denotes a favourable harvest ; and to the sailor that he will marry a rich widow.

PEARS.—To dream of pears prognosticates great wealth, and that you will be considerably elevated above your present situation to one of dignity and emolument. For a female to dream of pears, denotes that she will marry a person far above her rank, and she will live in splendour and happiness, notwithstanding her past ignoble condition. To persons in trade, this dream denotes success, the accumulation of wealth, and independency. It also foretells constancy in love and happiness in the marriage state.

PEARLS.—This is a very favourable dream, it foretells to the dreamer that by his own perseverance and
industry he will amass great wealth, and arrive at
great honours and dignities; that however poor he may
be at the beginning of his business life, he will die a
rich and great man, respected by the general public.
To dream that pearls are given to you, denotes a marriage with a very beautiful virgin, having an amiable
disposition and possessing great accomplishments, who
will make him very happy. If a maiden dreams that
some one adorns her with pearls, it foretells her marriage with a very rich man.

PEAS.—This is a good dream. To dream that you
are eating them, denotes great prosperity. If you
dream that you see them growing, it foretells good
fortune in love, and a happy marriage. To dream of
dried peas, foretells the acquisition of wealth.

PERJURY.—To dream that you have been guilty of
perjury, foretells your future imprudence, and want of
conscientiousness, which will expose you to contempt,
and subject you to neglect. This will reverse your
state, and reduce you to poverty and straits. It also
foretells sickness, troubles, and losses; and in love, the
unhappy choice of a partner for life; your children
will be a source of annoyance, being refractory and
disobedient, and not doing well. To the sailor it denotes suffering by shipwreck; and to the farmer very
bad crops.

PERFUME.—To dream that you are using a perfume,
or that you smell its rich fragrance, is always a favourable dream in reference to business, the seasons,
association, &c., and in love matters.

PHANTOM.—To dream that you see a phantom denotes that your expectation of the success of your

plans will be disappointed. Appearances may flatter you; but in vain. You think that you have secured the affection of your lover, but a rival will come and supplant you, and your lover will regard you with disdain. O be aware, of the contingency of human passions! It also denotes a quarrel with your best friend, which will cause you much sorrow. It also forebodes danger by travel, and loss of money by lending, and by giving too much credit.

PHEASANTS.—To dream that you see pheasants flying across your path, or in a field or plantation, it foretells that a relative or friend will leave you a legacy. If you dream that you see them fight, and fly away, you will be in danger of losing your legacy by a lawsuit.

PICTURES.—To dream of pictures is not good, it indicates falsehood and deceit. It matters not how beautiful the pictures may appear to you in your dream, it foretells your troubles arising from false and deceitful persons, who will malign your character, and restlessly try to damage your reputation. If you love any one, as your future partner, that person is false, however gracious and loving he or she may be. That person has been attracted by another, and they are only making you a tool to awaken jealousy and an endeavour to restore former intercourse. Therefore, labour, to ascertain *motives*. To persons who are married it foretells the infidelity of their partner.

PIGS.—To dream about pigs is the harbinger of a mixture of good and bad luck; it shows that you will have many false friends, but that you will have a sincere and faithful lover. It implies much sorrow and sickness, and that you will be exposed to great dangers, and especially to the danger of losing your life, but you will escape with a slight injury. It also forebodes that, notwithstanding many obstacles, you will rise in the world, and have a competency of worldly substance. But your children will be unfortunate; by their improvidence they will fall into poverty and disgrace.

PIGEONS.—To dream of seeing pigeons flying in the air or otherwise, prognosticates that you will receive important intelligence; they also denote a happy and suitable partner, and constancy and happiness in love. Also great success in trade, and the acquisition of wealth thereby.

PINE-APPLES.—To dream of pine-apples portends an invitation to a feast or wedding, where you will meet a person you will afterwards marry. You will marry well and happily, and have many fine children who will all grow up rich and respectable. It also foretells great success in business transactions. To the emigrant it bespeaks a safe voyage, and contentment and happiness in the country where he will settle.

PISTOL.—To dream that you hear the report of a pistol, foretells calamity coming upon you. If you dream that you are firing a pistol, it foretells that you will marry a person of hasty and passionate disposition, but very industrious. It also foretells that your marriage will be moderately happy; that you will have many children who will do well in the world; particularly the first-born who is sure to be conspicuous in the world, and be renowned for some great accomplishment or gift of nature.

PIT.—To dream that you are descending a pit shows that your business is rapidly declining, and that you will become the subject of want and distress. To a person in love it indicates the alienation of your lover's heart, and that he will treat you with cold indifference. To dream of falling into a pit, forebodes that you will be involved in misfortunes and troubles, and have many heavy losses; also that your lover or partner is unfaithful to you; and is actually permitting the advances of another lover, who, under the mask of friendship is wounding you in the most sensitive part. To a farmer it foretells bad crops, foul weather, and diseased cattle. After such a dream the merchant must meet with heavy losses, and the sea-faring man with disastrous weather, and terrible storms.

PLAY.—To dream that you are at a play, where you have much amusement betokens happiness in the marriage-state, and extensive success in trade. To a young man, or woman, it portends that they will marry well. To dream that you are taking part in a play, is not a good dream.

PLOUGHING.—For a young woman to dream that she sees a young man ploughing is a good omen, denoting that her future husband will be honest, sober, and industrious; and will by his own efforts and perseverance raise himself to independence. If a young man dreams that he is ploughing in a field, it foretells him that he will become very wealthy through his own exertions and industry. It also indicates much happiness in married life.

PLUMS.—To dream that you are gathering green plums, foretells much sickness in your family. To dream that you are gathering ripe plums in their season is a good dream for all. To dream that you pick them off the ground and they are rotten, denotes

false friends, and a deceitful lover, and also a change
in position, that you will fall into poverty and disgrace. If you dream that some one gives you ripe
plums, and you find them good to eat, it foretells
that you will have an agreeable lover, that you will
marry, and have a very comfortable home.

POISON.—To dream that you have taken poison
foretells a reversion in your circumstances; it denotes that your business will be unremunerating, that
you will suffer through the dishonesty of others, and
as a consequence be in poverty and distress. If you
dream that you recover from the effects of poison, it
is a sign that you will extricate yourself from difficulties, and do well. If you dream that another
offers you poison, it foretells a treacherous lover,
falsehearted, and foul ; but, though you will be disappointed in your first lover, you will soon get
another very much superior.

PRECIPICE.—To dream that you are on the edge
of a precipice is a dream to forewarn you to abandon
your present engagements and pursuits, for they are
sure to turn out disadvantageously and to your great
loss. After such a dream avoid taking a voyage or
journey, or you will repent it. Your lover is not
trustworthy, and you have seen some indications of
it; take warning, and after such a dream, renounce
the connection. In trade do not be too confiding;
if after such a dream, you trust your goods, or lend
your money, you are sure to be imposed upon.

PREGNANCY.—If a married woman dreams that she
is pregnant, it implies the birth of twins; and if a
young woman dreams the same, it denotes that her
sweetheart's motives are not honourable, and that he

has a design on her virtue, only wanting to make a meal of her.

PRISON.—To dream that you are in prison is a dream of contrary. It indicates freedom, happiness, unbounded scope in trade. In love, it foretells that you will marry a person whom you have known for a long time, but whom you have not regarded in the light of a lover. To dream that you are putting someone in prison, foretells that you will be invited to the wedding of an acquaintance or relative.

PROVISIONS.—To dream that you are hungry, and require provisions, and cannot obtain them foretells poverty and want. But to dream that you have abundance of provisions stored up implies a future state of competency, and in probability, it foretells a long journey, either by sea or land, and that you will be in many dangers; but that you will overcome them all, and in a foreign land acquire much wealth, and return with your abundance to your native land.

PUBLIC HOUSE.—To dream that you are keeping a public house denotes that you will be driven to extremities in your temporal affairs, and be compelled to act against your inclinations. To dream that you are drinking at a public house, is a bad omen, indicating sickness and poverty, and probably imprisonment for debt. In love it foretells cruel and deceitful treatment by a lover, who will very coolly abandon his attention towards you. In business it foreshows great losses. To sailors it foretells shipwreck and misfortunes; and to the farmer a great loss of crops through bad weather, and loss of cattle through the influence of epidemic disease.

PURSE.—If you dream that you find a full purse, it foreshows great happiness, particularly in love;

and that you will marry a person of great property by whom you will have a numerous family. To dream of losing a purse foretells your own sickness, or that of your lover.

QUADRUPEDS.—To dream that you see many quadrupeds of various kinds, portends that you will pass through a life of toil and labour, but in the end you will accumulate wealth, and be very happy and comfortable in your old age.

QUAILS.—It is an unlucky dream, denoting bad intelligence, and family jars. It also shows that you will lose your lover through false aud artful reports; it also foretells disasters at sea. It also tells you to beware of false and deceitful friends and lovers. It is not an omen of happy matrimony.

QUARRELS.—This is a dream of contrary; for if you dream that you quarrel with some person, it foretells success in business or in love, and that you will enjoy much wealth, and a married life, notwithstanding all opposition.

QUEEN.—To dream that you are in the presence of the queen foretells advancement to a honourable position in life. This will be effected principally by your efforts; also you will have many friends. To a young woman it shows that she will marry a person holding a high official situation in the state, that they will have a numerous family, and become very rich and happy.

QUICKSAND.—To dream that you are walking amongst quicksands, implies that you are surrounded with many temptations, and have many propensities to evil, and you do not know it. It is to be feared that you will run into many dangers through your own imprudence and hasty conduct, and thereby damage your reputation.

QUOITS.—Dreaming that you are playing at quoits indicates uncertainty in trade, and losses, and probably a reverse in your circumstances. It is to be feared that poverty will overtake you.

RABBITS.—To dream that you see rabbits implies that you will soon have to reside in a large and populous city, where you will marry and have a very numerous family. It also foretells that you will have a flourishing trade, that your plans will be successful, and that you will triumph over many enemies. For a married woman to dream of rabbits, indicates increase of family.

RACE.—To dream that you run a race on foot, betokens the defeat of your competitor; it foretells your success in business. You will secure the affections of the one whom you so ardently love. You need not fear a rival, you will marry and be happy.

RAFFLE.—This dream of chance foretells mean associations, and degraded habits. You will sustain the loss of character, the ruin of your business, and meet treacherous people, false love, and disappointment in matrimony.

RAIN.—To dream of rain generally foretells trouble, especially if it be heavy and attended with boisterous winds. To dream of gentle spring rain, is a very good dream, denoting prosperous circumstances, and happy love.

RAINBOW.—This is a token for good. It portends change, but a change for the better.

RATS.—To dream about rats, foretells many enemies who will cause you a great deal of trouble and anxiety, and by whom you will suffer many losses. In love it denotes a rival who has great influence over your intended, and who will leave no stone unturned to supplant you. You are in great danger from such evil designing persons. It is however the best to suffer the loss of a person who is not invulnerable to such specious baits. In matrimony it shows that some pretended friend is studying how to undermine your happiness and peace of mind.

RAVENS.—This is a bad dream. It declares that trouble is coming, that mischief is brewing; you will suffer through injustice, and have to contend with poverty and adversity, and have many sorrows. In love it shows that your lover is false, and your partner is to be suspected.

RICH.—To dream that you are rich is a dream of contrary. You will be poor for a long time; and only gain competency in the end.

RING.—If a married woman dreams that she loses her ring off her finger, it portends the infidelity of her husband, and that he is under the influence of a fallen female, who will ultimately ruin him. If a female dreams that her wedding-ring breaks, it foreshows the death of her husband; and if she dreams it presses her finger and hurts her, it forewarns her of the illness of her husband, or some of the family. To dream some one puts a ring on your finger, foretells union with the person you love.

RIVER.—To dream that you see a broad, rapid, and muddy river and tempestuous, it denotes troubles and difficulties in love and business; but if the river appears calm, with a glassy surface, it foretells great happiness in love, happy wedlock, beautiful children, and commercial prosperity.

ROSES.—To dream of roses in their season is the omen of happiness, prosperity, and long life. If the roses are full and fragrant, it foretells to a young man who dreams it that his mistress will be fair and beautiful, intelligent and amiable, and that their union will follow in due time, and be honourable and happy. It is a good dream for the tradesman and for all, prognosticating great success. If the roses are decayed, it indicates trouble and poverty.

SAILING.—To dream that you are sailing in a ship on smooth water, foretells prosperity; on a tempestuous sea, misfortunes. To sail to, and arrive at a pleasant country, denotes happiness in wedlock. To dream that you are sailing in a small boat, and that you gain the harbour, it foretells that you will make a rapid fortune.

SERPENT.—This foretells a deadly enemy bent on your ruin. If you are a lover, there is a rival replete with envy and malice, who will labour to displace you from the heart of your lover; indeed this serpent has already fascinated, and your star is beginning to wane; you are injured by artful insinuations, and base falsehoods. Let not such treatment destroy your peace and happiness. To dream that you kill a serpent, portends that you will vanquish your enemies and be successful in love, matrimony, and business.

SHAVING.—To dream that a person is shaving you, denotes a treacherous lover; and great disappointments; if you are married it denotes infidelity and discord; and to the man in business, it foretells losses.

SHEAVES.—To dream that you see a field full of sheaves of corn, denotes a favourable harvest, and a time of plenty. If you dream that you are gathering the sheaves into your own garner, it is a sign that you will acquire wealth by your enterprise. If you see the sheaves fallen down, in a state of confusion, it predicts a bad harvest, and a time of scarcity. To dream that you see fine corn in sheaves, and standing well, denotes to you prosperity, a very happy marriage, and beautiful, and obedient children.

SHEEP.—To dream you see sheep feeding is a portent of great prosperity and enjoyment. To dream you see them scattered, denotes that you will meet with persecution. To see sheep-shearing indicates riches, by marrying a wealthy person, this will make you independent of business.

SHIP, OR SHIPS.—To dream that you have a ship of your own sailing on the sea with merchandise, foretells your advancement to riches. To dream that you have taken a berth in a ship, and that you sail on the ocean, denotes that you will emigrate to a foreign country, where you will settle for a long time. To dream you land safely, and walk out with a person occasionally, it denotes that you will be married to a person in that country; that your union will be a happy one; you will have children, and amass great wealth, return to your own country, and live to a good old age. If you dream that you are in a ship, and it becomes leaky, it is a sign that your voyage will not be successful; If a woman enciente dreams about ships, it portends that her offspring will be a male, who will be engaged in a seafaring life.

SHIPWRECK.—To dream you suffer shipwreck betokens misfortunes. To a lover great disappointment in love. Your lover will be reduced in his circumstances, and unable to marry you. To a male it portends that the fair one will fall ill, and perhaps die. To dream that you see others shipwrecked, is a dream of contrary; you will see the elevation of some friends, or relatives.

SHOES.—To dream that you have got a new pair of shoes, is a sign that you will have to take many journeys. If you dream that your shoes hurt you, it denotes that you will be unsuccessful in your engagements. It is a bad sign for a lover. If you dream that your shoes take in water, it shows that you will be calumniated; it portends the falsehood of a lover. To dream that you are without shoes, denotes that you will pass through life with comfort and honour. To the lover it betokens virtue, sincerity, and ardent affection in your intended.

SHOOTING.—To dream that you are shooting a bird, and succeed, is very portentous. It denotes that the tradesman will accomplish his purpose; that the lover will secure the company and marriage with the person desired. But if you dream that you shoot and miss, is a bad portent. It denotes that in business you will be unsuccessful. The dream has the same prognostication to the merchant, the farmer, and the seaman. To dream that you shoot game foretells elevation to a state of wealth, and domestic happiness. To dream that you shoot a bird of prey is a sign that you will conquer your enemies.

SHOP.—To dream that you keep a shop is a sign of moderate comfort. You will have to succeed by industry and perseverance. To dream that you are serving with another person in a shop, indicates that you will meet with a conjugal partner of agreeable mind and manners; and that you will strive together most heartily, and at length succeed in acquiring an independency.

SILK.—To dream that you see silk, or buy, or sell silk, is an omen of good fortune to the tradesman. If the lover dreams of seeing a female in silk, it foreshows that his future wife will be wealthy and very agreeable, being most ardently and sincerely attached to him. If a female dreams she is dressed in silk, it foretells that her future husband will be in good circumstances, and that both will move in respectable society.

SILVER.—To dream that you are collecting small silver coins, foreshows distress; if large coins, you will be engaged in some lucrative trade. To dream that you are paying silver for goods which you receive, or of receiving silver for goods which you sell, denotes a prosperous trade, though but limited. To dream that you possess silver vessels, services, it foretells poverty; you will have to be content with earthenware, if you can get that. To dream that your silver turns out not real, foretells a false friend, or lover.

SINGING.—It is a dream of contrary, and foretells cause for weeping, and lamentation. It is portentous whether you dream you sing yourself, or hear others sing. The tradesman will suffer loss from his customers, the merchant will have no returns for the goods which he has shipped, and the sailor will have a very bad voyage through winds and storms, and the vessel in which he sails will become a wreck. If you love, it portends that the object will cause you to mourn by loving another in preference. To dream that you hear others singing denotes distress among your friends and relatives, and that you will suffer through their misfortunes.

SNAKES.—This dream denotes sly and inveterate enemies, who will conspire against you, and by whom you will suffer in your character and estate. It foretells that you will have a false lover, who will abandon you in a heartless manner. To dream that you destroy a snake, denotes that you will vanquish your foes, and all your rivals in love.

SNAILS.—To dream of snails, is not a very good dream. It foretells that you will be annoyed with very low evil-designing persons. Be watchful, lest you suffer through their designs.

SNOW.—To dream that you see the ground covered with snow is a sign of prosperity, and that you will maintain an unblemished character in spite of the attempts of your foes to blacken it. To dream that you are walking upon snow with your intended, foretells that your intended will be very beautiful and good. To dream that you are in a snow-storm and very much harassed, is a good dream. You will have difficulties, and calumny; but you will overcome, and come out of the ordeal unscathed.

SOLDIERS.—To dream that you are a soldier, foretells that you will abandon your present employment, and change from one thing to another. It is a bad omen for a young woman; she will marry a worthless man, with whom she will experience much trouble. To the tradesman it prognosticates severe and heavy losses. To dream you see soldiers fighting, denotes that you will be concerned in some serious contentions.

SUN.—To dream of seeing the sun foretells success in obtaining wealth, and success in love. To dream that you see it rise, denotes good news; to see it set, disagreeable news to the tradesman and losses. To dream that you see the sun overcast, is a sign of troubles, and great changes.

SWEETHEART.—If you dream that your absent sweetheart is beautiful and attractive, is a sign of purity and constancy. If you dream that your sweetheart is pale and sickly, it is a sign of inconstancy, and probably of falsehood.

TEETH.—To dream that you see a person with white regular teeth, denotes that you will have a beautiful lover whom you will marry. To dream that your teeth are very loose, portends personal sickness; to dream that one of them comes out, denotes the loss of a friend or relative; to dream that they all fall out, is a sign of your own death. To dream that you have the toothache is a dream of contrary; it denotes much social enjoyment and pleasure. To dream that you cut a new tooth, denotes change of residence, and to the married an increase of family.

TEMPEST.—This dream indicates many troubles, and losses, but you will surmount them; and recover from them; much persecution, but your enemies can do you no harm. The lover need not fear rivalry, for the object beloved is superior to all temptation, however enchanting.

THIEVES.—To dream of thieves, is a bad dream; it denotes loss in all cases.

THORNS.—To dream of thorns, portends grief, care, and difficulties.

THUNDER.—To see lightning, and to hear loud

peals of thunder, implies that you will be exposed to hazard and danger, from which faithful friends will extricate you. You should be on your guard after such a dream. If you are pursuing any vicious course, you are, by your dream warned to abandon it immediately, or it will be your ruin. If you dream that you see lightning and hear thunder at a distance, it denotes that you overcome all the enemies and dangers that threatened you, and become very successful in business, and be very rich. All your speculations will be successful. So to the lover; he or she, however jealous and fearful in the past, shall succeed and grasp the prize in happy wedlock.

TOADS.—This dream, to a tradesman, denotes ill-disposed competitors in the same line of business, and determined opposition from them. For a lover to dream of a toad, or toads, foretells that the object of your affection is low and mean, undecided, and inconstant, and not invulnerable to the advances, of a flattering and deceitful person. To dream that you kill a toad, denotes success and triumph in all cases.

TOMBS.—To dream that you are walking among tombs, foretells marriages ; to dream that you are ordering your own tomb, denotes that you will shortly be married ; but to see that tomb fall into ruins denotes the reverse, and also great sickness and trouble to your family. To dream that you, with another person are admiring tombs, denotes your future partner to be very suitable for you. To dream you are inspecting the tombs of the illustrious dead, denotes your speedy advancement to honour and wealth.

TREES.—To dream you see beautiful trees in rich

and beautiful foliage, and fruit-trees in bloom, or full of fruit, augurs unusual prosperity in business, in farming, in commercial or maritime affairs. If a lover dreams of seeing trees in blossom, or fruit, it is the portent of a really good marriage, of this worlds goods, and numerous beautiful and virtuous children. To dream you see trees cut down intimates the loss of friends by removal, or death, and also losses in business. To dream of climbing trees implies that your course through this life will be up the hill difficulty.

TRUMPET.—To dream that you blow a trumpet is a sign of prosperity, and of the total discomfiture of your enemies who have striven hard to injure you. But if you dream that you hear the sound of a trumpet, it denotes coming trouble. Your competitors in trade will have the best of the race. You will have quarrels in your family, or with your relatives, or friends. You will hear of an insolvency which will tend greatly to embarrass you. And if thou art a lover, it is the trumpet of rivalry which thou hast heard; thy rival has conquered, and thou wilt soon know it.

TURKEY.—This is a showy bird, and to dream you see one, denotes instability in trade, and friendship. Let not the lover be attracted by gaudy appearance, for this dream portends union with a vain, irritable, and bad-tempered person. Therefore, be on your guard.

UNFAITHFUL.—To dream that your friend, partner, or lover, is unfaithful, is a dream of contrary; they will be just the reverse. But to dream that you are unfaithful, denotes the approach of some peculiar temptation which may put your profession of attachment to the test.

VAULTS.—To dream of being in vaults, deep cellars, or places under ground, signifies the loss of a lover, and matching with one who has been married before.

VERMIN.—To dream that you are infested with vermin foretells sickness; but if you dream that you get rid of them, restoration to health.

VIOLIN.—To dream that you hear the music of a violin, foretells some social gathering, at which you will be a guest. It may be a marriage, the birth of a child, or the return of a friend from a distant country. To see dancing with the music denotes prosperity; and also the wishes of lovers agreeably consummated in matrimony.

VIPER.—Can this be a good dream? certainly not. It indicates that you have many bad persons around you as enemies, who will strive to injure you. It denotes an unfaithful partner. Your lover is false-hearted, and will sting you yet, by the most disreputable conduct.

VISION.—To dream that you see a person in a vision, prognosticates the sudden and unexpected death of a person appearing to you. To dream you see places, property, valuables, in a vision, denotes disappointment, poverty and misery.

VOICE.—To dream that you hear merry voices, foretells distress and weeping. To dream you hear the voice of lamentation prognosticates cause for joy. To dream that you hear many voices in conversation indicates some joyous event.

VOLCANO.—To dream of a volcano, foretells great disagreements, family jars, and lovers' quarrels. If you are designing to revenge yourself on any one, the injury will fall upon yourself. You will have to rue such a disposition. To a man of commerce, it portends dishonest servants, and a robbery, or some sad convulsion. It also implies civil disorders. To lovers, it is a sign that all deceit, intrigue, base designs, on one side, or the other, will be exploded, and the designer will be branded with the contempt and execration, so justly deserved.

VOLUME.—To dream that you are reading a volume, denotes that you will acquire fame, perhaps literary fame. To open a volume you do not like, and you put it from you, implies insavory associates, and the performance of disagreeable business. If a person in your dream presents you with a volume which you much admire, it foretells an agreeable courtship which will terminate in joyful matrimony.

VOLUNTEER.—To dream that you are a volunteer, denotes that you will be a soldier, and be wounded, or lose your life in battle. For a female to dream that she is walking with a volunteer, is a sign that she will be married to a soldier.

VULTURE.—To dream you see a vulture, is a really bad dream. It is evident that some enemy or enemies are seeking to destroy your character and reputation. Let lovers beware. There is a rival malevolent and decided, determined to possess at all hazards, and determined to revenge.

WAGGON.—To dream that you are driving a waggon, is a sign of poverty; if the vehicle is your own, it foretells advancement. To dream of riding in a waggon portends loss of situation or loss of character and credit. If you dream that a loaded waggon comes to your door, foretells that some one will befriend you, by which you will be advanced in life.

WALLS.—To dream of walls as a barrier, and which you cannot climb, denotes great difficulties in trade, and much embarrassment in family affairs. If you see your lover on the other side of a wall, which you cannot get over, foretells that there will be insuperable difficulties in the way of your union. You will have to encounter the opposition of your lover's friends and parents; besides, the advances of a rival will cause hesitancy and oscillation. To dream that you walk on narrow walls and high, foretells dangerous enterprise; but to descend without injury, or the wall falling, denotes success.

WAR.—This is not a good dream. It foretells to the tradesman, much competition and rivalry in trade. To a family it portends an occurrence which will interrupt domestic peace and happiness. It indicates great mutation in health and in circumstances; poverty frequently following competency, and vice versa, and health often interrupted by sickness. If a female dreams about war, very likely she will be the wife of a soldier; and if a woman enciente dream of wars, it is a sign that her next male child will rise up to become a soldier.

WAREHOUSE.—For you, tradesman, to dream of being in a warehouse, predicts that you will succeed well in business, and obtain large possessions, through your indefatigable labour and exertions. It also foretells that the dreamer will marry a female having a considerable portion, and rear a very interesting family. To a merchant, farmer, and speculator, it is also a good portentous dream.

WEDDING.—To dream of a wedding, portends a funeral near you or among your relatives. To dream that you are married, is a dream of contrary, it denotes a life of single blessedness. For a sick person to dream of being married, foretells his death, and the same applies to a female. To dream that your lover is married to another, foretells that your lover will expose you.

WEEPING.—To dream that you weep is a sign that you will have cause for joy. In trade you will be very fortunate, and when you see the results of your enterprise, trade, or speculation, you will rejoice. You will be crossed in love, perhaps lose your intended ; but you will have cause to rejoice in a more amiable and loving friend. Your clouds, even in family trouble, have silver linings eventually.

WHEAT.—To dream that you see a field of ripe wheat, portends that you will grow very rich, and eventually retire independent ; that you will marry a rich and very beautiful person, by whom you will have a large family of interesting and intelligent children, who will be your comfort in life's sad decline. It predicts to the sailor that he will have a safe voyage, return home to marry a person of good fortune, which will qualify him to retire from the sea to live in affluence.

WIDOW.—To dream that you are conversing with a widow, foreshows that you will lose your wife by death. For a woman to dream that she is a widow, portends the infidelity of her husband. For a young woman to dream that she has been married, and become a widow, prognosticates that her lover will abandon her.

WIDOWER.—To dream that you are one, denotes the sickness of your wife. For a young woman to dream that she is married to a widower, denotes much trouble with false hearted lovers: but she will be happily married at last to a man of sense and good conduct.

WIFE.—To dream that you are a wife portends you will not be one. For a man to dream he sees his wife, portends her sickness, but she will recover.

WIND.—To dream of a brisk wind, denotes joyful tidings. To dream of strong stormy blasts denotes trouble in all states, and crosses in love.

WINE.—To dream that you are drinking wine, portends health, wealth, long life, and happiness. To dream that you are drinking wine with other persons in great hilarity, foretells your wedding-feast. You will marry the person who has captivated your heart. If you are married, this dream denotes that you will have many children, who will reverence and honour you. If you are in trade you will find it very lucrative, and eventually you will retire independent. This dream also indicates that the troubles of a family will be short in duration, and be followed by high enjoyment.

WREATH.—To dream that you have a wreath upon your head, denotes the conquest of difficulties, and the successful enterprise of trade, to a lover, it denotes union with a superior parson, and great festivities on that account. All will be followed by permanent happiness, except the common ills or infirmities to which poor humanity is always liable.

YEW-TREE.—This dream denotes the death of an aged person, or relation, or patron, from whom you will possess a legacy which will place you above want. If you dream that you sit under a yew-tree, it foretells that your life will not be long. But if you merely gaze upon it, and admire it, it is a sign that you will live long.

YOUNG.—To dream of young persons is a sign of domestic enjoyment. To dream that you were once young, is a sign of your sickness. To dream that you have become young again, is a sign of your approaching dissolution. For young persons in love to dream of their childhood, is the precursor of agreeable courtship, with very loving persons, and ultimate marriage.

Sun Lore of All Ages: A Survey of Solar Mythology, Folklore, Customs, Worship, Festivals, and Superstition, by William Tyler Olcott. ISBN 1-58509-044-1 • 316 pages • 6 x 9 • trade paper • $24.95

Nature Worship: An Account of Phallic Faiths and Practices Ancient and Modern, by the Author of Phallicism with an Introduction by Tedd St. Rain. ISBN 1-58509-049-2 • 112 pages • 6 x 9 • trade paper • illustrated • $12.95

Life and Religion, by Max Muller. ISBN 1-885395-10-8 • 237 pages • 5 1/2 x 8 1/2 • trade paper • $14.95

Jesus: God, Man, or Myth? An Examination of the Evidence, by Herbert Cutner. ISBN 1-58509-072-7 • 304 pages • 6 x 9 • trade paper • $23.95

Pagan and Christian Creeds: Their Origin and Meaning, by Edward Carpenter. ISBN 1-58509-024-7 • 316 pages • 5 1/2 x 8 1/2 • trade paper • $24.95

The Christ Myth: A Study, by Elizabeth Evans. ISBN 1-58509-037-9 • 136 pages • 6 x 9 • trade paper • $13.95

Popery: Foe of the Church and the Republic, by Joseph F. Van Dyke. ISBN 1-58509-058-1 • 336 pages • 6 x 9 • trade paper • illustrated • $25.95

Career of Religious Ideas, by Hudson Tuttle. ISBN 1-58509-066-2 • 172 pages • 5 x 8 • trade paper • $15.95

Buddhist Suttas: Major Scriptural Writings from Early Buddhism, by T.W. Rhys Davids. ISBN 1-58509-079-4 • 376 pages • 6 x 9 • trade paper • $27.95

Early Buddhism, by T. W. Rhys Davids. Includes *Buddhist Ethics: The Way to Salvation?,* by Paul Tice. ISBN 1-58509-076-X • 112 pages • 6 x 9 • trade paper • $12.95

The Fountain-Head of Religion: A Comparative Study of the Principal Religions of the World and a Manifestation of their Common Origin from the Vedas, by Ganga Prasad. ISBN 1-58509-054-9 • 276 pages • 6 x 9 • trade paper • $22.95

India: What Can It Teach Us?, by Max Muller. ISBN 1-58509-064-6 • 284 pages • 5 1/2 x 8 1/2 • trade paper • $22.95

Matrix of Power: How the World has Been Controlled by Powerful People Without Your Knowledge, by Jordan Maxwell. ISBN 1-58509-120-0 • 104 pages • 6 x 9 • trade paper • $12.95

Cyberculture Counterconspiracy: A Steamshovel Web Reader, Volume One, edited by Kenn Thomas. ISBN 1-58509-125-1 • 180 pages • 6 x 9 • trade paper • illustrated • $16.95

Cyberculture Counterconspiracy: A Steamshovel Web Reader, Volume Two, edited by Kenn Thomas. ISBN 1-58509-126-X • 132 pages • 6 x 9 • trade paper • illustrated • $13.95

Oklahoma City Bombing: The Suppressed Truth, by Jon Rappoport. ISBN 1-885395-22-1 • 112 pages • 5 1/2 x 8 1/2 • trade paper • $12.95

The Protocols of the Learned Elders of Zion, by Victor Marsden. ISBN 1-58509-015-8 • 312 pages • 6 x 9 • trade paper • $24.95

Secret Societies and Subversive Movements, by Nesta H. Webster. ISBN 1-58509-092-1 • 432 pages • 6 x 9 • trade paper • $29.95

The Secret Doctrine of the Rosicrucians, by Magus Incognito. ISBN 1-58509-091-3 • 256 pages • 6 x 9 • trade paper • $20.95

The Origin and Evolution of Freemasonry: Connected with the Origin and Evolution of the Human Race, by Albert Churchward. ISBN 1-58509-029-8 • 240 pages • 6 x 9 • trade paper • $18.95

The Lost Key: An Explanation and Application of Masonic Symbols, by Prentiss Tucker. ISBN 1-58509-050-6 • 192 pages • 6 x 9 • trade paper • illustrated • $15.95

The Character, Claims, and Practical Workings of Freemasonry, by Rev. C.G. Finney. ISBN 1-58509-094-8 • 288 pages • 6 x 9 • trade paper • $22.95

The Secret World Government or "The Hidden Hand": The Unrevealed in History, by Maj.-Gen., Count Cherep-Spiridovich. ISBN 1-58509-093-X • 203 pages • 6 x 9 • trade paper • $17.95

The Magus, Book One: A Complete System of Occult Philosophy, by Francis Barrett. ISBN 1-58509-031-X • 200 pages • 6 x 9 • trade paper • illustrated • $16.95

The Magus, Book Two: A Complete System of Occult Philosophy, by Francis Barrett. ISBN 1-58509-032-8 • 220 pages • 6 x 9 • trade paper • illustrated • $17.95

The Magus, Book One and Two: A Complete System of Occult Philosophy, by Francis Barrett. ISBN 1-58509-033-6 • 420 pages • 6 x 9 • trade paper • illustrated • $34.90

The Key of Solomon The King, by S. Liddell MacGregor Mathers. ISBN 1-58509-022-0 • 152 pages • 6 x 9 • trade paper • illustrated • $12.95

Magic and Mystery in Tibet, by Alexandra David-Neel. ISBN 1-58509-097-2 • 352 pages • 6 x 9 • trade paper • $26.95

The Comte de St. Germain, by I. Cooper Oakley. ISBN 1-58509-068-9 • 280 pages • 6 x 9 • trade paper • illustrated • $22.95

Alchemy Rediscovered and Restored, by A. Cockren. ISBN 1-58509-028-X • 156 pages • 5 1/2 x 8 1/2 • trade paper • $13.95

The 6th and 7th Books of Moses, with an Introduction by Paul Tice. ISBN 1-58509-045-X • 188 pages • 6 x 9 • trade paper • illustrated • $16.95